THE COMPLETE IDIOT'S GUIDE TO

Selling Your Crafts on Etsy

Selling Your Crafts on Etsy

by Marcia Layton Turner

ALPHA

A member of Penguin Group (USA) Inc.

ALPHA BOOKS

Published by Penguin Group (USA) Inc.

Penguin Group (USA) Inc., 375 Hudson Street, New York, New York 10014, USA • Penguin Group (Canada), 90 Eglinton Avenue East, Suite 700, Toronto, Ontario M4P 2Y3, Canada (a division of Pearson Penguin Canada Inc.) • Penguin Books Ltd., 80 Strand, London WC2R 0RL, England • Penguin Ireland, 25 St. Stephen's Green, Dublin 2, Ireland (a division of Penguin Books Ltd.) • Penguin Group (Australia), 250 Camberwell Road, Camberwell, Victoria 3124, Australia (a division of Pearson Australia Group Pty. Ltd.) • Penguin Books India Pvt. Ltd., 11 Community Centre, Panchsheel Park, New Delhi—110 017, India • Penguin Group (NZ), 67 Apollo Drive, Rosedale, North Shore, Auckland 1311, New Zealand (a division of Pearson New Zealand Ltd.) • Penguin Books (South Africa) (Pty.) Ltd., 24 Sturdee Avenue, Rosebank, Johannesburg 2196, South Africa • Penguin Books Ltd., Registered Offices: 80 Strand, London WC2R 0RL, England

International Standard Book Number: 978-1-61564-245-8
Library of Congress Catalog Card Number: 2012949173

15 14 13   8 7 6 5 4 3 2 1

Interpretation of the printing code: The rightmost number of the first series of numbers is the year of the book's printing; the rightmost number of the second series of numbers is the number of the book's printing. For example, a printing code of 13-1 shows that the first printing occurred in 2013.

Printed in the United States of America

Note: This publication contains the opinions and ideas of its author. It is intended to provide helpful and informative material on the subject matter covered. It is sold with the understanding that the author and publisher are not engaged in rendering professional services in the book. If the reader requires personal assistance or advice, a competent professional should be consulted.

The author and publisher specifically disclaim any responsibility for any liability, loss, or risk, personal or otherwise, which is incurred as a consequence, directly or indirectly, of the use and application of any of the contents of this book.

Most Alpha books are available at special quantity discounts for bulk purchases for sales promotions, premiums, fund-raising, or educational use. Special books, or book excerpts, can also be created to fit specific needs. For details, write: Special Markets, Alpha Books, 375 Hudson Street, New York, NY 10014.

Publisher: *Mike Sanders*	**Cover Designer:** *Rebecca Batchelor*
Executive Managing Editor: *Billy Fields*	**Book Designers:** *William Thomas, Rebecca Batchelor*
Senior Acquisitions Editor: *Brook Farling*	**Indexer:** *Johnna VanHoose Dinse*
Senior Development Editor: *Christy Wagner*	**Layout:** *Ayanna Lacey*
Senior Production Editor: *Jan Lynn*	**Proofreader:** *Jan Zoya*

Contents

Appendixes

Introduction

Etsy is one of the fastest-growing retail websites around. Whether you're in search of a place to sell your handmade crafts or you already have an Etsy shop and want to know how to sell more, you've come to the right place.

Whereas eBay pioneered the consumer-to-consumer online marketplace, Etsy has taken that idea one step further. Instead of selling anything to anyone, as eBay essentially enables you to do, Etsy is specifically for artisans looking to connect with buyers who appreciate life's finer things. From art to knitting to woodworking, blown glass, handmade jewelry, sewed pieces, papier-mâché, and more, you can find—or sell—it on Etsy.

Successful selling on Etsy starts with your crafts. Maybe you have a stash of pieces you've created but don't know what to do with, or maybe you've recently discovered a crafting technique you love and want to use to make some money. All you have to do is set up shop, show your work to potential customers, and provide excellent customer service.

I wrote this book to help you create your Etsy storefront and find success selling on this virtual marketplace, whether you're an Etsy newbie or a seasoned pro. There's always something new to learn that can make your product listings more appealing, drive more traffic to your Etsy shop, and help expand your customer base. I designed this book to help you with all these things—and more. In it, I show you the ins and outs of Etsy and help you avoid making the same rookie mistakes most sellers have already made.

Throughout you'll find stories and lessons learned from seasoned Etsy pros who make part or all of their income from the site. Many sellers are part-time, investing time in their craft after working a full-time job or after the kids are in bed. Others have worked their way up to selling full-time on Etsy, which provides the bulk of their income. Others simply enjoy selling on Etsy when they find the time to craft, doing so more for the enjoyment than the revenue.

Whatever category you fall into—aspiring full-time Etsy seller or more casual—you can pick up ideas for selling more with less effort in the following chapters. Here's to your success!

How This Book Is Organized

This book is organized into five parts, followed by a series of appendixes with additional resources to turn to.

Part 1, Getting Started with Etsy, is designed to help new or would-be sellers find their niche on Etsy. You might be the world's best at a particular kind of craft, but unless you have a market interested in buying it, you may waste your time crafting. On the other hand, if you find that a particular kind of item is selling like hot cakes, you may be able to make some serious money by giving buyers the crafts they want. In Part 1, you learn how Etsy functions, get tips for researching what's currently selling—on Etsy and in other marketplaces—and discover how to protect yourself once you uncover a hot product category.

Part 2, Setting Up Shop, is probably the most important part of the book. To be profitable on Etsy, you need to set up your Etsy shop properly, establish policies that demonstrate to buyers you're legitimate without setting yourself up to be scammed, specify how you want to be paid, and create a packing and shipping process that wows buyers without costing you an arm and a leg. This behind-the-scenes work isn't always exciting, but it will make the difference between a hobby and a business.

Part 3, Selling 101, delves into what you need to do to separate your crafts from your competition on Etsy. Just making a superior product isn't enough—you need to price it competitively, describe it in terms that will make buyers swoon, and photograph it to highlight its beauty. On top of that, you also need to keep careful records of your crafting process to be sure you're making money and not just spending it, which is easy to do if you're not paying attention.

Part 4, Marketing Your Etsy Business, shows you the many ways you can market your Etsy shop outside the Etsy community. Sure, Etsy provides a wealth of ways to connect with fellow sellers, get feedback and advice, and help support each other as business owners, but that's only part of the marketing story. Thousands of other tools and techniques are available to allow you to make contact with potential buyers, both online and off. Part 4 points you to some of the most effective tricks of the trade to save you time and money while boosting your business reputation.

Part 5, Growing Your Business, helps you look beyond Etsy to plan for the next phase of your crafting career. Some of the most successful Etsians have found the website to be a truly effective stepping-stone to new, bigger opportunities. This part helps you start to map out your business plan, if you hope to one day sell on a larger scale. And not all Etsy sellers do, to be honest. Many are content to create at their own pace and sell when they feel like it. You can do exactly that, or you can explore what might lie beyond Etsy's walls.

In the back of the book, I've included a glossary of terms used in the book and sometimes on Etsy along with additional resources—websites and other materials—to turn to for ideas and support in growing your Etsy business.

Added Extras

Throughout the book, I've added extra bits of information you'll definitely want to check out. Here's what to look for:

CRAFTY TOOLS

Check here for useful suggestions, online sites, and mobile apps that can save you time or improve your marketing results.

DEFINITION

These sidebars cover important Etsy definitions and terminology.

WATCH OUT!

You can save yourself frustration and grief by paying attention to these cautionary notes.

Acknowledgments

Thanks go to publisher Marie Butler-Knight for her commitment to producing an Etsy book for serious crafters. Brook Farling was instrumental in making this book a reality, providing helpful assistance and guidance along the way that certainly made the manuscript stronger. Christy Wagner helped ensure the copy was error-free and visually pleasing—thanks, Christy! And literary agent Marilyn Allen was my champion, as always, helping persuade Alpha I was the right Etsy seller for the job.

I also owe a big thanks to the many Etsy sellers who were willing to be interviewed about their art and their success on Etsy. I really appreciate your time and input, Vickie Anderson, Erika Boetsch, Elizabeth C., Nicole Cherry, Matt Cipov, Benjamin John Coleman, Courtney Gifford, Hannah May Halleck, Christine Hwang, Karen Juneau, Kathy Kambic, Abby Leigh, Kim Piotrowski, Lisa Ratcliff, Morgan Roberts, and Michael Jon Watt.

Thanks, too, to my family, for their patience as I spent days and nights writing, writing, writing.

Special Thanks to the Technical Reviewer

The Complete Idiot's Guide to Selling Your Crafts on Etsy was reviewed by an expert who double-checked the accuracy of what you'll learn here, to help us ensure this book gives you everything you need to know about setting up shop on Etsy. Special thanks are extended to Julie Corbett.

Julie blogs at On the Dot Creations (onthedotcreations.com), where she combines her love of polka dots with her admiration for all things handmade. She lives in North Carolina with her childhood sweetheart, Jon, and her son, Mason. Her hobbies are taking photographs, singing in church, dabbling in graphic design, and reading books with her son.

Trademarks

All terms mentioned in this book that are known to be or are suspected of being trademarks or service marks have been appropriately capitalized. Alpha Books and Penguin Group (USA) Inc. cannot attest to the accuracy of this information. Use of a term in this book should not be regarded as affecting the validity of any trademark or service mark.

Getting Started with Etsy

Etsy is one of the fastest-growing websites, both in terms of revenue and traffic. Etsy sales were up 67 percent in 2011, with more than 800,000 active shops and more than 17 million members. It's no wonder craftspeople and artisans are flocking to this online marketplace for handmade items.

By providing a platform for artists to market and sell their work, Etsy has hit on something big. An increased concern for the earth, cost-conscious consumers, and a backlash against all that is commercial created the perfect opportunity for Etsy, and for crafters.

Fortunately, it's not difficult to tap into this demand for the handmade. But before you start listing your works of art, you need to be prepared. Study the market to spot what's hot right now and what will be soon. Identify where consumer demand overlaps with your offerings. And then take steps to ensure your work remains unique and free from copy-cats.

Say Hello to Etsy

In This Chapter

- The ease of Etsy
- Etsy's impressive growth
- Etsy's plusses and minuses
- Standing out from your competition

Painter/carpenter/photographer Rob Kalin conceived Etsy, "the world's handmade marketplace," in 2005. At the time, there was no established marketplace for creative artisans to sell their works online. Sure, there was eBay, but buyers were more likely to head there for cell phone accessories and hard-to-find toys than for hand-carved wooden furniture or pastel landscapes. So Kalin and two colleagues, Chris Maguire and Haim Schoppik, decided to build such a website from the ground up. Within 90 days, Etsy.com was up and running.

Just a few short years later, Etsy is now *the* place for all things handmade. Crafters who knit, make jewelry, blow glass, carve wood, sew, quill, paint, embroider, weld—you name it—are finding success at selling their handiwork on Etsy.

In this chapter, you learn why Etsy has become *the* place to be if you're a crafter looking to sell your creations. I also share some online tools that can make listing and selling your pieces faster and easier.

How and Why It Works

Etsy brings buyers and sellers together by allowing craftspeople to create online product listings describing their handmade items and post them on Etsy.com. There, buyers can search the vast database of items by word or phrase, such as *leather belt* or *glass vase*, in search of handmade items.

When shoppers find a piece they want to own, they can immediately buy and pay for it online, which alerts the seller to pack and ship it to the buyer.

Today, craftspeople and artisans who formerly relied on sales at local festivals and crafts fairs for income can market their goods to the world, all thanks to Etsy. Many Etsy sellers are part-time, but increasing numbers of crafters are able to make a full-time living via the site.

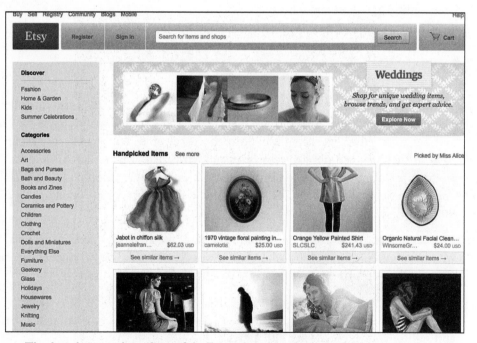

The clean design and simplicity of the Etsy website has won kudos from buyers and sellers alike.

Rising Popularity

For a website established less than a decade ago, Etsy's traffic and sales figures are impressive. As of summer 2012, Etsy had more than 15 million members and more than 875,000 active shoppers. Sure, they haven't yet overtaken eBay, which has 100 million active users, but few other online marketplaces can claim such a large customer base.

Benjamin John Coleman (etsy.com/people/Benagami) was selling pieces of origami bonsai on eBay and making a decent living when he read an article in *The New York Times* in 2008 about Etsy. He joined that day, figuring at $.20 a listing, "Etsy was a no-brainer" for his $40 to $50 paper sculptures. Coleman's initial efforts paid off big, and he was consistently profitable—although his main reason for setting up an Etsy shop was for the exposure, not the money.

After creating a new art form, Benjamin John Coleman leveraged Etsy to spread his origami bonsai worldwide.

(© Benjamin John Coleman)

Between 2011 and 2012, Etsy had a 74 percent increase in revenue growth, climbing from $180.6 million to $314.3 million in a single year as a direct result of increased seller success. Sellers sold more products, which boosted the company's income. In fact, $525 million worth of merchandise was sold on Etsy in 2011, and more than 13 million were items listed.

Isn't it time you list some of your handmade items on this rapidly growing online retail site?

Why Buyers Flock to Etsy

Etsy is perhaps the anti-eBay, the antithesis of mainstream collectibles, fad items, and cheap knock-offs. Precisely because it is devoid of mass-produced products, consumers find the site appealing. They appreciate being able to support skilled artisans and purchase items they won't see in their local Walmart.

Etsy is a popular destination for gifts. Knowing that the recipient of an Etsy gift likely has never seen it before—and doesn't already have two—is another bonus to savvy shoppers. The reasonable prices don't hurt its appeal, either.

The combination of unique, quality, handmade, and reasonably priced is a winner for Etsy buyers and sellers alike.

The Artist's Marketplace

Where crafters could only connect with buyers in person at events, such as juried arts festivals, craft fairs, and fund-raisers, Etsy provides a way for sellers to immediately market their offerings internationally. The world is their market, and the sales potential is enormous.

Why You Need to Be Here

I'm not suggesting you stop participating in craft festivals, but know that Etsy is an additional source of revenue you shouldn't ignore. Selling on Etsy reduces the time you need to invest to make a sale—there's no need to pack up, set up, and man a booth in the blazing sun. What's more, you can be selling your fabulous creations while you sleep. Once you list your work, you can sit back and let Etsy bring buyers to your shop.

Granted, it probably won't happen overnight. Figuring out the best way to describe and photography your items takes practice, but over time, and with the tips and techniques I share in this book, you can build a solid following. As your customer base grows, so will your sales.

Selling Smart

Etsy isn't the pot of gold at the end of the rainbow, and not everyone who lists their handmade goods makes money. In many cases, it's not because their product was poor, but because they didn't invest enough time to learn the Etsy listing process. It's not difficult, and if you follow the suggestions I offer in these pages, you'll be in good shape.

Too many sellers finish a new painting or a set of earrings and want to list it for sale ASAP. They are so pleased with their creation, they whip through the listing, not realizing their lack of attention will seriously reduce their chances of ever selling their painting or pair of earrings.

Etsy takes patience, and you need to take time to follow the step-by-step instructions and recommendations Etsy offers for creating a product listing. You also need to be patient while waiting for sales to come in. Some sellers expect that as soon as their new listing is live and visible on Etsy, sales will come rolling in. Rarely is it that immediate.

Even if buyers see your listing, they may decide to wait. Maybe they wait to see what other pieces you put up for sale, or maybe they continue shopping and compare your piece with other sellers' they come across.

Etsy isn't always a quick sale, but it can be a consistent source of income if you become a consistent seller. That means regularly creating new pieces, listing them for sale in your shop, routinely checking your shop stats to see what terms buyers are searching for, retaking photos you decide are subpar, and relisting pieces that haven't sold yet.

Keep in mind that the lack of an immediate buyer doesn't mean your pieces are overpriced. It's more likely that they're *underpriced*, to be honest. (For more on pricing, see Chapter 9.) Be sure each and every piece you sell generates a profit for you. Even if you love what you do, there's no reason you should take a loss on any items you sell.

What Sells

If you knew what would sell well on Etsy, you'd probably be able to sell more, wouldn't you? Knowing in advance what buyers want to buy gives you an advantage during your creative and production process.

> **CRAFTY TOOLS**
>
> To get a sense of what types of products are selling, you can peruse a shop's list of sold items. Search as if you were a buyer, looking for shops that sell items similar to yours, and study their sold items. You can't see how much a buyer paid, but you can certainly get a sense of what buyers like by studying your competition.

Determining What Categories Are Selling

For a preview of what types of products, styles, and colors will be big sellers this month, read the "Seller Handbook" on the Etsy blogs. From the Etsy home page, click **Blogs** and then **Seller Handbook**.

Etsy also puts out occasional "Merchandising Desk Reports" regarding what's expected to sell well in the coming months. For example, here's one for the holiday 2011 season: etsy.com/blog/en/2011/from-etsys-merchandising-desk-november-2011.

Etsy analysts carefully track what's selling; what isn't selling; and what fashions, materials, shapes, and colors are predicted to be popular. Then they prepare a comprehensive report of what's expected to do well in the coming weeks and post the information on the Etsy blog.

If you've been selling on Etsy for more than a couple months, you also have historical data from your own shop you can refer to. Take a look back at your own past sales to note the typical demand curve. If you have a seasonal product, such as Christmas wrapping paper, you should be able to spot when demand for it began to rise, when it peaked, and when it became nonexistent last year. Use that helpful information to determine where you should invest your time and energy now. And if your sales show your Christmas wrapping paper won't be hot again for several months, spend your time on items more likely to be snapped up now.

Looking at Price

Unfortunately, there's no way to search completed sales to see how much particular items sold for. However, by creating a list of your closest Etsy competitors and watching their inventory, you can learn a lot about what price point is most popular, discover how long it typically takes for an item to sell, and gauge approximately how much profit they're making.

Nicole Cherry (etsy.com/shop/cherrycoaccessories) started selling her handmade jewelry, including popular zipper bracelets and necklaces, a few years ago, but she jumped on the Etsy bandwagon only a few months ago. Before making the leap, Cherry did a lot of research, studying existing Etsy shops, to be sure her pieces were different enough from what was already there. She also made note of her competitors' prices, to be sure she could come in slightly lower. So far, so good, she says. "Each week that goes by, my views and [number of favorites] are increasing"—a sign interest and demand are on the rise, too.

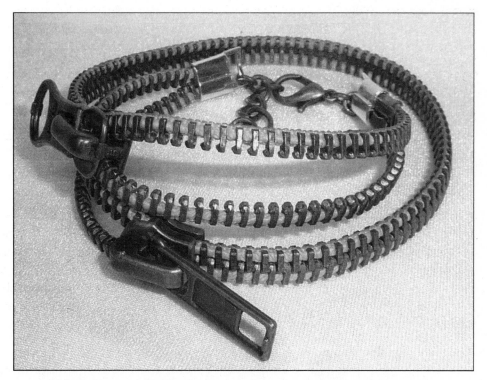

*Nicole Cherry studied her Etsy competition and strategically priced her zipper
jewelry at or below the market rate.*

(© CherryCo)

You can also turn to other websites to see what similar products are selling for. Granted, they won't be the exact same thing because your items are handmade, but if you headed to eBay, for example, you can conduct a completed listing search to see how much, in general, similar items to yours are selling for. That can give you a ballpark idea of the range you should charge for your pieces.

Completed eBay listings give you a sense of what buyers there have paid for products similar to your own.

Pros and Cons

If you're wondering whether it's really worth the time to set up a shop on Etsy, let's take a quick look at the advantages and disadvantages of being there.

Pro: Remote Sales

The biggest advantage of selling on Etsy, and anywhere online really, is the ability to make sales without having to be personally present. No standing in a booth or sitting by a table answering questions from buyers at a craft fair all day.

By selling through an established website, you enjoy targeted traffic—buyers who are already interested in handmade goods—that you don't have to attract on your own. Etsy does that for you. All you have to do is have your pieces listed and available for sale when buyers come to your shop.

Pro: Low Fees

By comparison to virtually any other sales venue—online or offline—Etsy is cheap. You pay $.20 to list an item for 4 months or until it sells, whichever comes first. When it does sell, you pay Etsy 3.5 percent of the sale price.

Those fees, including listing and transaction fees, are billed monthly, and sellers have until the fifteenth of the following month to pay via credit card or PayPal.

By comparison, on eBay, you pay between 7 and 13 percent when your item sells. There's no fee to list or to sell on Craigslist, but your market is limited to those in your local area, whereas Etsy and eBay reach a global audience.

Etsy lets you keep so much more of what you earn, which is a big plus.

Con: Lesser-Known Site

Although Etsy has certainly grown exponentially in the last couple years, it still has a much smaller customer base than eBay, Craigslist, or Amazon. Fifteen million members is nothing to sneeze at, but Etsy is dwarfed by eBay's 100 million. Similarly, many consumers have never heard of Etsy, much less shopped there.

There's huge upside potential, but be aware that Etsy is still a relative newbie.

Con: Restricted Categories

Etsy also has a much broader list of restricted product categories—products it prohibits from being sold on the site. All retail websites have items they don't allow, such as Nazi paraphernalia or counterfeit designer purses on eBay, or alcohol on Amazon. But Etsy wants only a specific type of product. It's easier to explain what it *does* allow than what it doesn't.

WATCH OUT!

Etsy maintains a list, albeit fairly brief, of prohibited items. Find it by clicking **Help** on the home page, clicking **Site Policies**, and choosing **Prohibited items** from the list. Most are obvious—weapons and live animals, for example—but others are left to the sellers' discretion. Etsy also reserves the right to remove listings it feels fall under this prohibited category.

Etsy only wants three types of products:

- Handmade items

- Vintage pieces—these don't have to be handmade

- Supplies—these are components for handmade items but don't have to be handmade themselves

If your product is mass-produced or purchased from another distributor or retailer, it's not considered handmade. However, if you assemble or piece together machine-made items, Etsy considers the item handmade. The distinction is that you added some value yourself by hand.

The definition of vintage varies slightly depending on the product involved, but Etsy defines vintage as anything more than 20 years old. Most collectors consider vintage furniture as being 30 to 100 years old. However, vintage clothing is typically apparel made between the 1920s and 1960s.

Supplies can be almost anything used to make something else by hand. They can be new or used. So new canvases, new paints, new brushes, new beads, and new yarn are all fine. Used pieces of jewelry, used fabric, used patterns, and just about anything else new or used that's legal to resell are okay, too.

Staying Competitive

As Etsy adds buyers and sellers, competition continues to heat up. Whereas in Etsy's early days, 50 sellers may have specialized in handmade leather journals, but these days, there might be 500 or 1,000.

More sellers bring more buyers intrigued to explore what creative products are available on Etsy, but sellers then need to remain vigilant about setting themselves apart from the rest. With increasing competition comes the need to become more and more distinctive, either in product design or packaging or service.

WATCH OUT!

As you look for ways to be successful on Etsy, do not copy what another seller is doing. Copying someone else's design is a copyright violation that can cost you tens of thousands of dollars. So feel free to mimic a seller's process or packaging approach but never their product.

Of course, increased competition is not a reason to pass up Etsy—far from it. The opportunities are there, but the sellers who take steps to set themselves apart rake in the bulk of those sales. Be one of those sellers.

The Least You Need to Know

- Etsy sold more than 13 million items in 2011, generating sales for crafters of more than $525 million—that's a market every crafter should want a piece of!
- Etsy offers crafters a way to sell without having to be present, man a booth, or travel to a craft fair.
- Becoming successful on Etsy takes practice, study, and patience, but the potential returns are large.
- To stand out from your competition, you need to look for ways to make your shop and your crafts eye-catching.
- Etsy's charges exceptionally low fees to sell compared to other larger online retailers.

Understanding Your Market

In This Chapter

- Discovering what's popular
- Finding a niche
- Getting in sync with what's selling
- Planning for seasonal shifts

If you're thinking about selling on Etsy simply as a way to generate a little cash from your hobbies, know this: you'll sell more of anything you make if you tap into popular trends. Making what you know consumers want yields far more sales than making whatever you want and hoping there's a market for it. It's much smarter to find where your interests and skills intersect with what customers want. Fortunately, all you need to do is uncover the current trends.

The good news is that once you spot those trends, you can adapt your creations to cater to those buyers and sell more of your wares. A number of tools alert you to the hottest colors, styles, shapes, materials, and products, so you can adjust your own inventory to mirror what's expected to sell well.

In this chapter, you learn more about identifying what's selling and what's not. There's nothing worse than investing hours and hours creating something that has no chance of ever selling. You want to avoid that, and this chapter gives you tips for spotting what's going to sell well.

Trendspotting

Trendspotting, also called trendwatching, is big business, and companies pay consultants to research and report on what consumers will be buying in the upcoming months. With that information, companies can more effectively anticipate what will be hot next week, next month, or next year. They can then stock up on the right inventory and sell more to their customers. It's like shooting fish in a barrel, as they say.

> **DEFINITION**
>
> **Trendspotting,** or *trendwatching,* is all about predicting the next big thing. Knowing what buyers will be looking for on Etsy in the coming weeks and months can be helpful as you decide how to invest your time in crafting new items to list.

Predicting the Next Big Thing

Trends don't magically appear out of nowhere. They build, they develop, they crescendo, and they expand, but they most certainly don't just instantly arrive full-blown. For a trend to get started, many factors on several fronts all trigger to cause a trend to develop.

What does this mean for you? It means you can pick up on trends as they begin to form. By monitoring a number of different information sources, you can piece together the emergence of coming trends.

One great tool to help you do this is Etsy's newsletters. Check out the latest style trends in its twice-a-week Etsy Fashion newsletter, stay current with popular products on the daily Etsy Finds newsletter, and hear from other sellers in Etsy Success. Sign up for any or all of these newsletters by clicking **Your Account** on the home page (when you're logged in), clicking the **Settings** link, and opening the **Emails** tab.

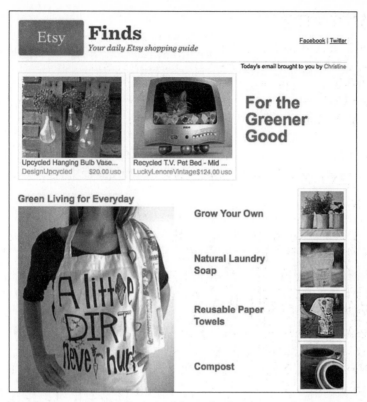

The Etsy Finds newsletter delivers useful trend information right to your mailbox.

Getting Ahead of the Curve

To be one of the first to spot trends, you need to combine information from the best sources to be able to identify changes across several fronts. These sources include but are not limited to the following:

News media. Read, or at least skim, the top stories in magazines related to your craft or industry, as well as the leading business magazines and newspapers, association bulletins, websites, and leading bloggers and thinkers. What are they talking about? What do they predict will change how we live in the next few years? What are the disruptive technologies we should be watching? If you find topics being discussed in several industries or media, that's a tip a trend may be emerging.

For example, you read in *The Wall Street Journal* that the cost of platinum has fallen relative to silver. (It hasn't; I'm just making it up as an example.) If you're a jeweler, that should be a tip-off to start designing with platinum because your consumers might soon want those pieces.

Colleges and universities. Although professors don't usually drive trends, they do notice and study them, making them a good source of information when you want to identify emerging trends. Many universities publish newsletters about faculty research you can read. Or you can search university websites to see who specializes in subjects you're interested in and check out their perspective on the topic.

For example, you find a study out of the University of Michigan saying college students are buying fleece underwear like crazy. (Again, I'm making this up.) That information should give savvy Etsy tailors and seamstresses an idea.

Networking organizations and websites. Pay attention to the topics your friends, colleagues, and contacts are buzzing about. This is good advice at business meetings, on LinkedIn and Facebook, as well as at the supermarket. What is everyone discussing? What are they concerned about? When you start to hear the same conversation over and over in different settings, you may have stumbled on a product about to make it big, or an opportunity in the making.

At a recent small business conference, perhaps you noticed several entrepreneurs were using teak tablet cases. (Again, this is a completely fictional example.) You might do a little online research to see if this is a local trend, if it's an emerging trend, or if Best Buy simply clearanced all its teak computer accessories last week.

Catalogs. Direct-mail catalogs are another tool for spotting what's heating up. Flipping through retail catalogs on a regular basis helps you gauge which colors are hot, which styles are big, and which products are at the tipping point of becoming trendy.

The fabrics hawked by J. Jill and Eileen Fisher this season might be a jumping-off point for a new shawl or jacket, for example. Or the accessories shown in this season's Pottery Barn catalog might spark an idea for a new handmade line of similar home décor items before the trend gets huge.

Personal experience. Sometimes the best way to understand the market's newfound fascination with a product or service is to personally experience it. Order the new iPad everyone is talking about if you can afford it, or buy that hot app. What is it that consumers are responding to? That's at the heart of the trend.

You can gather a lot of competitor intel by sampling how other Etsy sellers serve their buyers. If you make small purchases from several sellers, you may be able to identify trends related to packaging and communication, for example.

Kim Piotrowski (etsy.com/shop/kipi), who sells her original gouache paintings on old book pages and prints on Etsy, bought a number of items early on from other Etsy sellers "to see how other artists package their works, how quickly shipments are sent, and how much communication occurs." She found that Etsy sellers often include a little freebie with their order, a practice she has now adopted.

Buying from other sellers helped Kim Piotrowski improve her own business selling paintings like this and spot trends among other artists on Etsy.

(© Kim Piotrowski, kipi.etsy.com)

Google Trends. Leave it to Google to build a tool for identifying trends as they happen. Log into google.com/trends to see what search terms are hot today and check how much traffic certain search terms are generating.

Hot searches on any given day might include celebrity names, sport MVPs, computer viruses, breaking health news, and so on. Tomorrow might have a whole set of new terms.

Checking in regularly can help you spot big trends, especially when you see the same terms over and over, or several related terms.

CRAFTY TOOLS

Companies in a wide variety of industries often issue annual predictions. PANTONE, the color company, does its own *PANTONE Fashion Color Report* that includes the shades expected to be big sellers each spring and fall season. Find it at pantone.com.

Sometimes it's hard to tell which trends are on their way up and which are falling out of favor. For that, you need to do a little research, checking to see if the search term has reached its peak or is on its way down. By itself, however, one piece of information really can't tell you if it's a hot trend or not.

What's Hot/What's Not

One of the best places to start studying potential trends—and identify which products and services are falling out of favor—are best-seller lists. Many online retailers track sales of their products and report on how well each is selling. *The New York Times* and *The Wall Street Journal* both have their own best-selling book lists. And Amazon and eBay both publish updated lists of their hottest-selling items.

Google and other websites release regularly updated lists of trending words, phrases, and topics. Just by perusing these for a few minutes a day, you should be able to get a good idea of what people are talking about. That's the first step to identifying popular products you might find success selling.

Uncovering Popular Product Niches

Etsy is a somewhat close-knit community, but if a fellow Etsy seller stumbles onto a hot niche, they're probably not going to tell you about it. They're more likely to keep it to themselves and cash in on the trend. However, you can still discover popular product niches using CraftCount.com. If you click the **Top Sellers by Category** tab and then click **Handmade** in the **Main Category** box, you'll see a list of the top Etsy sellers, ranked by total sales.

Learn who the top Etsy sellers are, look at what they're making their money on, and see if you can cash in on some of that business.

With the name of each Etsy shop, you can then do some research on the top 50 to 100 shops to learn what they're selling that buyers are responding to—and spending money on.

Etsy Tools for Finding What's Selling

Unlike some sites that only share information about what's hot with their top sellers, Etsy is an equal opportunity community that routinely shares information about current and anticipated trends with anyone paying attention.

The best place to turn to for guidance regarding current and future trends impacting Etsy is its blog. This post from May 2012, titled "From Etsy's Merchandising Desk," looks ahead to June and reports on what's trending, so sellers can start creating merchandise that sells: etsy.com/blog/en/2012/from-etsys-merchandising-desk-june-2012. Each month, Etsy releases a similar report on what's hot now. It also highlights upcoming events that may spur sales, which you can center a promotional campaign around in your own shop if you want.

Here are some other tools you can use specific to spotting craft trends:

> **Yahoo! Groups** (groups.yahoo.com). Join groups of like-minded crafters on Yahoo! to learn about what's popular and what's up-and-coming in your particular part of the crafting world.

> **Craft and Hobby Association** (CraftandHobby.org). Even if you don't attend the association's annual conference for crafters, you can see what they plan to talk about, which is a good sign of what's hot now.

> **Pinterest** (pinterest.com). The internet's latest darling website, Pinterest is another tool for monitoring what consumers are responding to. Look to see what images are the most pinned.

> **Etsy Treasuries** (etsy.com). Yes, treasuries are compiled by other sellers, but they're also a look at what someone else thinks is new and fresh. The ones you see on the home page are often onto something.

eBay Hot Lists. Just as Etsy reports on what's hot in handmade, eBay reports on what's selling, and what's not, on the online auction site. For example, to see a list of what eBay expected to be hot for holiday 2012, from the eBay home page, click the **Sell** link in the top-right corner, choose **Seller Information Center** from the drop-down menu, click **Essentials** on the left side of the page, and the Holiday Selling Guide is a clickable link under that header: pages.ebay.com/sellerinformation/sellingresources/holidayhotlist2012. html.

Matt Cipov is always testing new products, such as this one, to see which are in greater demand with buyers than others, so he can create more of what sells and less of what doesn't.

(*Owls of the Deep #1, © 2010 Matt M. Cipov*)

WATCH OUT!

Be careful that the trend you think you've identified isn't really a fad. A trend can have a long-term impact in a number of areas, while fads are extremely short-lived. The popularity of animal prints continues to spread as a fashion and style *trend,* while Snuggies, for example, may be a *fad* product without much long-term growth potential.

Another smart tactic is to test out new craft ideas on a small scale before investing large sums in raw materials. Matt Cipov (etsy.com/shop/mattycipov) stresses that because Etsy has identifiable sales cycles, it's important to "always be testing." Some times of the year are always busy, while others are typically slow. For that reason, you want to be sure you're well stocked for the periods when Etsy is bustling. Because the listing fees on Etsy are so affordable, Cipov points out, it's to your advantage as a seller to take low-risk tests in listing new items, trying out new directions, or putting up something to gain real-time Shop Stats. This will help you see if the item is gaining the attention or views you had hoped for. Then invest your time and energy in the listings that are garnering attention while testing other ideas you have.

Seasonality

Every business has its busy season(s) and its quieter times, and Etsy is no different. Depending on your particular niche, your busy and quiet seasons may be completely different from other sellers'. You may be busy during the lead-up to the winter holidays while other sellers do their biggest months toward the end of the school year.

Knowing when to expect a surge of orders is helpful for inventory planning, so you can use the slower times to prep for the craziness.

Apply the trend information you've gathered to create a list of expected hot sellers, and start stockpiling those items to list as your busy season approaches. Or if you have more than one busy season, or an inventory that changes with the seasons, be sure you're always modifying your available products to match what your buyers are looking for.

The Least You Need to Know

- Trendspotting, or paying attention to what's going on around you, gives you a better picture of what products will be hot in coming months.
- Reading reports from Etsy, eBay, and Google can clue you in on what shoppers are increasingly looking for.
- To refresh images of products in your inventory, retake photos using different, seasonal backdrops or season-appropriate props.
- Use trend information to anticipate and prep for your shop's busiest seasons, creating inventory to have on hand for when business picks up.

Creating Inventory That Sells

In This Chapter

- Learning what buyers want
- Standing out in a crowd
- Buying raw materials cost-effectively
- Keeping your inventory organized

The key to success in business—whether you're selling on Etsy, at craft festivals, or in your own store—is to sell what people want. You could be the best brewer of dandelion tea around, but if no one wants to buy it, your skills are wasted. So before you amass an inventory of tea, or lightweight balsam wood chairs, or fancy feather headdresses, stop and take stock of what buyers on Etsy want. What exactly are they willing to spend their hard-earned dollars on?

Once you have a sense of what they want to buy, you can determine what kind of inventory you should create and how best to stand out among the competition. Although you may perceive your products to be completely unique, odds are very good some other Etsy sellers have crafted something mighty similar, or have something that can function in place of your item. So instead of aspiring to be (or convincing yourself you are) the only supplier of your type of craft on Etsy, figure out a way to stand out and become the *preferred* seller.

In this chapter, I give you ideas for finding raw materials so you can spend more time crafting and less time searching for supplies. I also share some suggestions for creating crafts that will stand out on Etsy. Etsy is growing, and more shoppers visit the site each day. However, as the site grows, it gets harder for your work to get noticed. This chapter can help.

Differentiating Your Products

When online buyers arrive at your Etsy shop, either by keyword search or through a Treasury, you want to do your best to make your store and your crafts really shine. Your listings need to be different in at least one way to make your creations more appealing than similar items out there. You can distinguish your work in several ways, but you really only need to choose one or two differentiators to sway buyers to buy from your shop.

WATCH OUT!

There's a saying that clients can have two of the following: speed, quality, or price. They can't ask for a top-quality product quickly if they aren't willing to pay a premium for it. Keep this in mind as you zero in on what makes you and your crafts unique. Don't try to be the highest-quality, lowest-cost, *and* speediest crafter out there. It's not a profitable niche. Choose two.

Features

One of the ways you can differentiate your creations is through their features. Some of your item's unique features might include the following:

- What it's made of
- Where those materials come from
- Its size
- Its number of components or pieces
- The techniques you used to create it
- How long it takes you to make one
- The colors you use
- How long it lasts

Of course, there are a million other potential product features, such as reliability, weight, and price, to name a few.

Before you can begin to compare your crafts against the competition, you need to make a list of your work's key features. Then make a list of the competition's product features. When you do a side-by-side comparison, can you see areas where you can set your crafts apart from the rest?

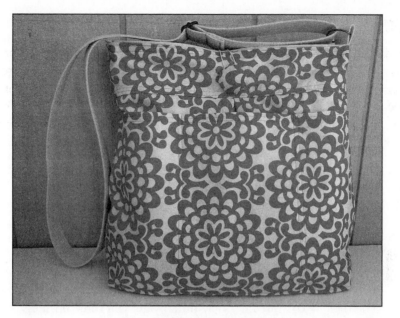

(© Lisa Ratcliff, Wild Sprout Design)

(© 2012 Pollywogs and Tadpoles)

These two gorgeous diaper bags both come up in a search for the term, but their features such as size, color, and material, are quite different as are the words used to describe them.

Can you find a different material to work with? Can you create items composed of more pieces? Can you work in colors that are hard to find in your craft specialty? What are your opportunities to really make your pieces stand out?

If you have no luck finding a way to differentiate your product from the rest, look to other features of your Etsy purchase process. Can you ship faster? Can you personalize your product at no additional charge? Can you provide more background information on where the raw materials came from? Read how your competition is describing their products as a starting point for finding ways you can do a better job at some aspect of the crafting or selling process.

Pricing

Differentiating your crafts by price is probably what you thought of first. After all, price is one of the top three things buyers look at when shopping. But do you go low, or do you go high-end?

Aiming to be the low-cost provider may initially get you some business. *Initially.* But do you want to establish your brand as the cheapest around? You could, and buyers who are price sensitive will appreciate having to spend less with you.

On the other hand, positioning your work as higher quality and deserving of a higher price tag is another way to separate your pieces from the crowd. Some buyers will prefer your work simply because they equate higher prices with higher quality or better workmanship.

Whether you opt to go higher-end, be competitive, or go lower-priced should depend on how your items stack up against the competition, what it costs to produce them, and what your buyers have suggested they would be willing to pay (based on what you've charged in the past). You can always change your pricing if you don't feel your current price tags aren't working for you, but just know that it's much easier to lower your prices than it is raise to raise them. (Unless, that is, you have more demand than you can keep up with. Then you can raise your prices until orders slow down.)

(© MadisonCraftStudio.etsy.com)

(© Courtney Gifford, Lovebugs Jewelry and Lip Balm)

These two necklaces look fairly similar and equally gorgeous, but they have different price points. The second necklace is much less expensive.

Packaging

Although buyers don't typically make a first purchase with the product's packaging in mind, you can certainly decide to carve out your own niche using a special method of packaging to separate yourself from other sellers. (I share ideas on how to be creative and memorable in Chapter 8.)

If you opt to go this route, you should consider highlighting the attractive packaging materials you'll use when preparing a purchase for shipment in the item description. Tell buyers what they can expect when they open the shipping box. Get them excited about the care you'll take when wrapping their new purchase. Perhaps one of your five listing photos could be of your creation in its packaging finery.

Keywords

I talk more about strategic use of keywords in Chapter 11, but for now, just know that your choice of words to describe your items can also differentiate you crafts from your competitors'.

Sure, you want to use some terms that are obvious and are likely to put you in front of customers searching for a "leather briefcase" or "marble bookends," for example. But don't be content with being matched only for the obvious terms buyers are using.

To break away from the competition, do some research using Google AdWords Keyword Tool (adwords.google.com/o/KeywordTool) to check out what more obscure words buyers are using in conjunction with the obvious ones. Using our "leather briefcase" or "marble bookends" example from earlier, using Google AdWords, you might find searches like "black brushed leather briefcase backpack" or "small marble bookends of children's storybook characters."

You can't really anticipate what terms buyers are using, but when you find the ones that are a bit less popular, less mainstream, you can weave them into your product description and catch those sales.

You don't need to register for AdWords to use the free tool, although you do need a Google account, which is also free.

How Much Inventory Do You Need?

Now that you've thought about how to make your creations stand out, how many should you create? How much is too little, and how much is too much? There's no one definitive answer here. What's right for you depends on how quickly your items sell. But in general, you want to have about 100 items for sale in your shop at all times in order to be ranked higher in Google. A higher Google ranking means your Etsy listing is likely to get seen by more shoppers. The lower the ranking, the fewer the shoppers who will be directed to your listing.

Past Sales Figures

The best way to determine how many items to stock at any one time is to review how many products you've sold in the past, and at what rate. Do you typically sell two items a day, a week, or a month? Depending on the pace of your sales, you can decide how many crafts to make and list.

Also keep in mind that relisting unsold items is a good way to bring them up to the featured listings again, so you might not need to continually be crafting if you can recirculate some of the inventory you already have in your shop. You pay 20¢ for a 4-month listing, but you can relist items an unlimited number of times. And there's no limit to how many listings you can have at one time.

Production Capacity

If your goal is to have around 100 items in stock and listed at all times and you sell 4 items per week, you need to make about 4 pieces every week to stay even. Is that pace reasonable for you? Given how long it takes you to finish a piece and what other demands you have on your time, is this a realistic production capacity for you?

If you're just getting started and want to work up to 100 items in stock, it's probably worth your time to calculate how long each piece takes to produce and how many hours per week you have to craft. Then create a production schedule that helps you reach your goal in a reasonable amount of time.

If you're gung-ho and want to be fully stocked in a week, you'll need to create at least 15 pieces a day. That may or may not be physically possible, depending on the complexity of your crafts.

> **CRAFTY TOOLS**
>
> If building a large inventory quickly is important to you, you could hire helpers to work alongside you or to handle one part of your production process. This will enable you to get more products completed in less time, but remember, you'll have to pay these folks for their help.

Sources of Raw Material

In addition to calculating your work speed and desired inventory level, you need to take into account your raw materials. Do you have enough on hand to complete all the products you want to? Do you have enough money to buy more materials so you can fill your stock?

If you have some funds available to invest in raw materials, let's look at how you can get more for your money by buying smart.

Retailers

Small Etsy sellers frequently purchase their supplies from retailers because they can buy in small amounts as they need materials. It's very convenient to buy what you need when you need it, and in quantities as small as one piece.

Etsy crafters rely on well-stocked craft stores like Michaels, Jo-Ann, Hobby Lobby, and A.C.Moore. Retail prices are higher than other raw material sources, but most local craft retailers issue weekly coupons for 40 to 50 percent off, which can significantly reduce raw material costs. If you don't currently receive coupons in the mail from your local craft retailer, sign up in-store or online to be added to the mailing list. Those coupons can save you a lot of money!

Craft retailer websites can be a great source of raw materials, craft ideas, and money-saving coupons.

Wholesalers

A step down from retailers in terms of cost are wholesalers, who sell to retailers. That means their prices are as much as 50 percent below retail costs. The downside is that you may need to buy in larger quantities to qualify for wholesale pricing.

To discover the appropriate wholesalers for your needs, contact the manufacturer of components you use—anything from paintbrushes to beads to fabric or sheets of metal—and ask about wholesale purchases. The company may refer you to your local wholesaler or agree to sell to you directly.

Distributors

Distributors and manufacturers, the original source of materials, may be able to offer you the lowest pricing. *May* is the operative word here because their contracts with wholesalers may prevent them from selling to you directly, cutting out the middle-man, who is their partner. You may have to be willing to buy a truckload of product to get the lowest prices. And do you really have space for that many supplies?

Unless you have an assembly line process in place, a warehouse, and a high demand for your items, it's likely you won't want to invest in the large quantities distributors demand. But it can't hurt to ask. Contact the manufacturer you'd like to work with to see what kind of pricing terms and quantities they'd be willing to give you. Perhaps you can negotiate a deal that costs less than wholesale pricing but only requires you to buy a little more than your wholesaler would. It's possible—you won't know until you ask.

Online

A few years ago, the list of potential suppliers would have ended with distributors, but today you have access to many of the same companies the major corporations do, thanks to the internet. You also have access to sellers who do business only online through websites like Etsy, eBay, Amazon, and more niche sites specific to your product category.

On eBay, for example, search for the word *lot* along with the item you're looking for to find supplies in larger quantities. Or do a Google search for your supplies using the description of your needed material plus the word *wholesaler* or *distributor.* You'll likely get a list of wholesalers who deal in the material you're after. From there, you can make contact and decide if a deal makes sense.

CRAFTY TOOLS

One of my favorite sources of low-cost raw materials is ShopGoodwill.com, the online arm of Goodwill Industries, the thrift store. I've found boxes of sterling silver, huge art canvases, and box lots of famous-name handbags there, all for a fraction of the retail cost. Don't overlook online thrift stores for raw materials and vintage items.

Organizing Your Inventory

After working so hard to create pieces to list in your Etsy shop, it's important to keep track of where everything is.

Sure, when you have one or two dozen creations, finding the particular item you just sold isn't hard. But when you have multiples of that, matching the item to the buyer can be challenging. And it can jeopardize your customers' satisfaction if you can't locate and ship their purchase in a timely manner. You really need to have an inventory management system.

Your Etsy Space

It's best if you can dedicate space to your Etsy business, rather than squeezing it into spaces around your home. Finding completed items later will get tricky—and time-consuming—if you've divided your pieces and stored them in several places within your home. So if you can, designate a bookcase, a table, a corner, a shelf, or a closet to all things Etsy.

Then devise a way to sort and store your items so retrieving the piece you just sold takes seconds instead of hours and doesn't require you opening every package on the bookcase, table, etc. to view the contents.

Chris Hwang, of ChrisCreatures (etsy.com/shop/ChrisCreatures), is a plush artist with a rapidly growing fan base. She puts her completed plushes together in one spot and when something sells, she packs it up for shipping. Having all her plushes in one place makes it easier to spot the particular plush that's been bought.

Keeping Good Records

Keeping physical track of your product is important, but having a database of your items is an important part of the process, too. An Excel spreadsheet is probably the easiest way to keep track of key pieces of information, such as the following:

- Item name and description
- Date listed
- Price set
- Product cost

- Etsy listing number
- Item location
- Date sold
- Sold price
- Profit/loss
- Days to sale

Having a database of all this information also comes in handy when you need to cross-reference products, compare costs, or look up materials used earlier, for example.

Organizing by Number

Perhaps the simplest way to organize your Etsy items is by number—the item number Etsy assigns when you create a listing. Because your biggest concern should be sending your customer the exact piece he or she ordered, identification is key.

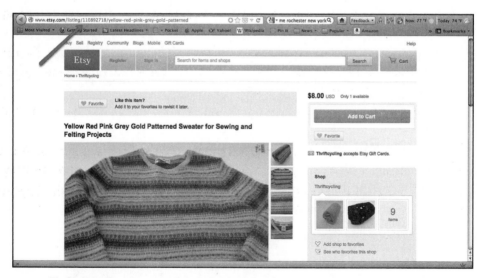

To find the Etsy item number, look at the number that appears in the item URL, following the word listing. *The item number in this example is 110892718.*

If you've taken the step of prepping your crafts for shipment, you really don't want to have to undo all that work to double-check what's inside the box. Instead, it's a good idea to print out a copy of your listing page and attach it to the box or shipping bag. This way, you'll be able to verify the item number and also check the item description before you head to the post office.

Organizing by Category

You can also organize your inventory by product category. If you only craft one type of product, this system might not be the best for you. In that case, I'd stick with organizing by the Etsy item number.

But if you sell several different kinds of pieces, such as pillows and rugs and blankets and hats, separate your items into the respective category so that when an order comes in, you know immediately where to find it. Attaching a print-out of the Etsy listing still makes sense here, even when you're able to zero in on its location quickly.

The Least You Need to Know

- Before creating inventory for your Etsy stop, check out what's already selling to see what buyers want to spend their money on.
- With millions of visitors flocking to Etsy, you need to find a way to make your creations stand out from the rest, or create shop practices and policies to give yourself a competitive advantage.
- Paying retail for raw materials makes sense if you only want a few supplies at a time.
- As demand for your crafts grows and the production pace quickens, seek out wholesalers, distributors, and online sellers for lower prices on raw materials.
- Keep your shop inventory in one location, labeled with a copy of the Etsy listing page so you can track it down quickly when you sell it.

Copyright 101

In This Chapter

- What does copyright protect?
- Is fair use fair?
- Reporting copycats
- Preventing copyright violations

The good news is that Etsy has become quickly known as the place to shop for quality, creative, handmade products. The bad news is that some of the people visiting the site actually come there to steal, not shop. They're stealing other artists' ideas and designs and claiming them as their own. Does that mean you should avoid Etsy altogether? No, not at all.

Etsy is a marketplace, much like a mall or retail store, nearly anyone can enter. Most shoppers are there in search of something handmade for themselves or to give as a gift. Others are competitors checking out the merchandise to see what's selling. (You've done that, too, right?) So although every shopper may not turn into a paying customer, the only way to possibly earn their business is to be where they're shopping.

In the long run, being on Etsy will make you more money than avoiding the site altogether. However, you still need to be aware of your rights should you discover someone is copying you.

In this chapter, you learn more about how to handle people who copy your work, how to protect yourself from such stealing, and what exactly a copyright does for you.

Your Rights as the Artist

One issue that's come up on Etsy in the last couple years is copyright. As the creator of a handmade product of your own design, you own the copyright. As owner, you possess six exclusive rights:

The right to reproduce the work. If you so choose, you can photocopy photographs you've taken and sell them, have giclée prints made of a large mural you painted, or sew duplicates of a dress you designed. Only you have the right to do that. Others need to get your permission first.

The right to distribute the work. If you made it, you can sell it wherever you want without restriction. Or you can give others permission to sell it. But others can't sell your works without your okay.

The right to create derivative works. The creator of a work, whether it's a poem, a drawing, or a song, is the only person who can take major sections of a creation and reuse them in a different way. A song that contains a chorus from another song running through it in the background, for example, is a derivative work and requires permission from the copyright owner.

The right to publicly perform the work. This mainly applies to music, choreography, plays, and movies, but the individual who conceived the idea and wrote it down is the only person who can arrange a performance. Others must have permission.

The right to publicly display the work. In the same vein as the right to perform the work, you also have the right to present a show, such as an art show or a movie. Others cannot copy your work and present it without your permission.

The right to publicly transmit audio performances. If you own the copyright to the recording of a song, radio stations have to have your permission to play it.

What Is a Copyright?

So what, exactly, is a copyright? It's a federal law that provides artists and craftspeople the right to control the use of their creative products—what they create. Unless you transfer your copyright to another person or company, you make all the decisions about how and where your design or creation is used, shown, performed, etc.

The length of time you own the copyright varies by country, but in the United States, a copyright term for works created after January 1, 1978, is the life of the author/creator plus 70 years. So if you create something this year, you hold the copyright for 70 years after your death.

WATCH OUT!

If you're hired to create a "work made for hire" for a client, such as with a custom order, you are agreeing to transfer the copyright and all ownership interests to the client. So if you want to retain the copyright, do not agree to work-made-for-hire arrangements. Or consider charging a higher fee for the work in those situations.

What Can Be Copyrighted?

The U.S. copyright office has identified eight categories of works that can be copyrighted:

- Literary, musical, and dramatic works
- Pantomimes and choreographic works
- Pictorial, graphic, and sculptural works
- Sound recordings
- Motion pictures and other audio-visual works
- Computer programs
- Compilations of works and derivative works
- Architectural works

Most original designs crafters put to paper will likely fall in the "pictorial, graphic, and sculptural works" category.

Michael Jon Watt, of TransitDesign (etsy.com/shop/TransitDesign), was the first U.S. artist to sell authentic-looking bus scrolls on Etsy. When others copied his work, he could prove he was the first artist creating the scrolls and, therefore, had copyright protection. Consequently, Etsy took down the work of the copycats and the artists were prohibited from making bus scrolls that were a clear violation of Michael's designs.

Michael Jon Watt's work was copied, until he took action to stop it.
(© Michael Jon Watt)

The key here is that you have to *commit it to paper* or computer media. Just thinking about it or imagining it doesn't give you copyright protection.

WATCH OUT!

Since March 1, 1989, including an official copyright notice on works has been optional. So just because you don't see a © symbol doesn't mean the work is in the public domain. You'll need to do more digging to uncover a document's or drawing's copyright status. On your own work, it's a good to add a copyright notice to be able to prove willful infringement. In a lawsuit, that could mean you win higher damages.

What *Can't* Be Copyrighted?

Ideas can't be copyrighted. You can copyright the expression of an idea in a particular form, such as a letter or article, but you can't copyright similar ideas other crafts-people come up with.

So if you decide that making bracelets out of sheets of music is a great idea, you have every right to create and sell them. However, if other artists see or hear about your sheet-music bracelets, or come up with the idea on their own as they search for recy-clable materials, you can't sue them and claim copyright violation. Your idea is just that—an *idea*.

I'm not an attorney, so definitely check with one to verify this, but if you made brace-lets out of sheets of music and wrote a poem around the outside, you can copyright that *poem* and prevent anyone else from using those exact same words together. But you can't prevent someone else from using sheets of music, folded and shaped and assemble in the exact same way as yours, which means you probably can't protect your folded bracelet. That's a process, which is not copyright-protected.

Specifically, the U.S. copyright office says these things do not receive copyright protection:

> **Ideas, procedures, methods, systems, and processes.** You can't copyright a recipe's list of ingredients, for example, but you can copyright the exact way you instruct others to put them together.

Titles, names, short phrases, and slogans. These things can, however, be trademarked, which provides similar protection against copies. So while McDonald's can't copyright, "I'm lovin' it," they can trademark it and prevent other companies from using that phrase.

Facts, news, and research. For example, you can't copyright a calendar or reports that Columbus reached America in 1492.

Works in the *public domain*. In general, anything published before 1923 that hasn't had the copyright renewed, or anything published by the U.S. government, is considered in the public domain.

> **DEFINITION**
>
> The **public domain** is the realm in which material is free and clear for the public to use. A literary work in the public domain, for example, doesn't need copyright protection, either because it expired or because it never had it. It can be modified and rereleased by other individuals or businesses at will.

Works not fixed in a tangible medium of expression. Anything not documented in writing or by recording cannot be copyrighted. To receive copyright protection, you need to write it or type it or record it before you can claim it as your own.

The most important point in this list for you, as a crafter and an Etsy seller, is that ideas cannot be copyrighted. Only by documenting your design, concept, draft quote, or whatever can you protect yourself and your creative products.

Protecting Yourself

It's nearly impossible to prevent someone else from copying your work if they're dead set on doing it. However, you can set yourself up to be awarded significant money damages if the copycats are caught.

To do this, first you need to apply the copyright notice (©) to your work. This isn't required, but it puts others on notice so they can't claim later that they didn't know it was protected by copyright.

Second, formally register your copyright. Yes, you have to pay to register your copyright (as of this writing, it's $35 per item via online registration), but you'll be in a much stronger position to win damages (translation: lots of money) if someone ever does violate your copyright. Without that registration, you'll have an uphill battle.

Third, keep watch for violators. Unless you're paying attention, you may miss incidents of infringement. I talk about steps you can take to thwart copycats and keep an eye out for them in a minute.

> **CRAFTY TOOLS**
>
> Information is power, and sharing information with other artists and craftspeople when you discover copycats and plagiarism can only serve to empower other Etsy sellers. If you have a blog, tell your story. Put it on Facebook. Tweet about. The more you share, the more aware other artists are going to be about protecting themselves, too.

Registering a Copyright

There are some common misconceptions about how and when copyright comes into being. You don't have to register a copyright or have your work published for it to be covered under U.S. copyright law. It is automatically protected by copyright at the moment of creation. This is called a *common law copyright*.

> **DEFINITION**
>
> As an artist, your original design is protected by copyright the moment you create it. This is called a **common law copyright.** You need to take additional steps to protect that copyright, but you earn it as soon as you create.

Debunking Copyright Myths

The whole point of copyright is ensuring that artists, authors, and creative professionals benefit financially from the fruits of their labor. But somewhere along the line, some confusion has emerged about what is copyrighted material and when permission is required.

Here are some common myths about copyright rules:

If it's on the internet, it's in the public domain. Not true. Creative professionals do not give up their right to copyright protection by publishing something online. You still need to get permission to use material someone else has created.

Chris Hwang's Etsy business captured a lot of attention—and copycats— when she created the Tofu for Obama plush figure in 2008. Rather than focus on the copies, Hwang, whom you met in Chapter 3, invested her energy in new designs. Today, her work has been featured in art gallery shows and national magazines.

Chris Hwang's Tofu for Obama plush figure was a big hit—with buyers and with copycats.

(© Christine Hwang)

The small amount of material I'm using is covered by fair use. The fair use doctrine indicates that portions of another's work can be quoted and used with attribution, but there's no exact formula to indicate how much is acceptable and how much is too much. It also depends on how important the excerpt is relative to the whole. It's always smarter to request and get permission before pulling from someone else's works.

I'm not violating someone's copyright if I give credit. Not so. You still need the copyright holder's permission. They may not want you to share their work—with or without credit—and they are the only ones who get to decide. You can violate someone's copyright even with proper attribution.

The material I'm using is from an out-of-print book, so I'm okay. Maybe. Or maybe not. Just because a book is no longer being printed doesn't impact the copyright status; the author still retains the rights to the work. Generally, books printed before 1923 are in the public domain—but not always. They may still be protected by copyright in other countries.

In all cases, if there's something you want to copy, check with the originator of the product, whether it's a pattern or a drawing or a new font. You'll avoid trouble later on by requesting and receiving permission from the copyright holder.

Understanding what rights you own is also important, so you recognize when your rights have been infringed. That's the first step to protecting yourself and regaining control of your work.

Making It Official

To recoup damages if someone copies your work, you have to have formally registered it with the U.S. Copyright Office within 3 months of publication, such as with a book or article, or before you discovered an infringement. You can file online at copyright. gov/eco for $35; if you prefer to mail your registration in, it will cost you $65.

You can't sue for infringement of your copyright unless you've registered it. So if someone else copies your work, you can sue them only if you've already formally filed a copyright registration.

In addition, you can sue for *statutory damages* and attorneys' fees if you've registered your copyright. Otherwise, you can only sue for the actual damages you can prove you've incurred, which may be nothing.

> **DEFINITION**
>
> **Statutory damages** are set fines imposed based on an incident, rather than calculated based on damages. Copyright infringement carries with it statutory damages of $30,000 per incident, or $150,000 per incident if willful infringement is proven. The value of the item copied doesn't matter. The damages are the same.

Preventing Forgeries

The only way to prevent thieves from seeing your work is by not posting it online to begin with—on Etsy or anywhere else. Of course, this also negates any chance you have of making a living online. So obviously that's not the solution.

To sell online and still protect your original work, there are a few things you can do. Keep in mind, however, that a serious thief will almost always find a workaround to steal from you if he or she really wants to. Your challenge is to make it as difficult as possible. The more difficult you make it, the greater the chances the would-be thief will give up.

Foiling Copycats

One step some artists take to try to foil copycats and thieves from stealing their online images, for example, is to turn off the right-click capability. This prevents would-be thieves from right-clicking an image and downloading a copy. Unfortunately, this is pretty easy to get around.

Another techno-trick artists and crafters use—with moderate success—is shrink-wrapping. Essentially, you overlay your work with another image so when someone tries to copy your work to their hard drive, all they get is the overlaid image. It's not foolproof, but it does make the theft more difficult for the novice thief.

> **CRAFTY TOOLS**
>
> For an excellent tutorial on shrink-wrapping your online images, check out skinny artist.com/how-to-shrink-wrap-your-images.

Watermarking is a method used frequently with photography, but it can be used on any kind of image. Just like the watermarks paper manufacturers overlay onto their sheets of letterhead, image watermarking involves applying a word or phrase over top of a photo, so the owner of the photo is clear. One equestrian photographer who used to watermark his images with a © and his name now boldly uses, "Copyright violation," to make it clear the image hasn't been purchased.

You can easily add a watermark to your photos with Photoshop or PaintShop, or you can purchase a software program specifically for watermarking. Check out one of the many online tutorials to learn how to add a watermark for free. Skinny Artist shares one at skinnywp.com/2011/watermarking-your-images-for-free.

There are two schools of thought regarding watermarks. One is to make it big enough and bold enough that it can't be cropped out by someone trying to steal the image for their own use. However, when it becomes too large and dominant, the watermark can obstruct the view of your craft. That's a big downside.

The other school of thought is to add a watermark that does *not* interfere with the product image, which would make your item less likely to be included in a treasury or cited by a blogger. When watermarks become large and unattractive they provide greater protection against misuse, but on the flip side, they reduce the likelihood of someone else pinning it on Pinterest, for example, or otherwise promoting it.

Watermarks are easy to add to images, making it obvious when a picture has been stolen.

Of course, clients who pay for photographs or digital imagery receive images that are free of any watermark. The only time the watermark is applied is over images that have not yet been bought.

Unfortunately, if someone is determined to copy your handiwork, unless it's an exact replica, you'll have an uphill battle proving your case. And if a crafter takes your basic idea and tweaks it slightly with his or her own approach, it may be considered a totally new creation. Such is the case with online plagiarism. Software programs, called spinners, take articles and swap out the words with synonyms to create new articles using different words but the same content. The "new" articles considered original works and, therefore, not copies.

If you find other crafters are stealing your designs and replicating them exactly, it may be worth your time to hire an attorney, or at least to ask Etsy to remove the listings. But unless the item is a lookalike, you may spend thousands of dollars and still not win a lawsuit. That's what you'll need to weigh when you come across copies—and given Etsy's expansion, it's likely that at some point you will see copies of your work.

Monitoring Your Competitors via Keyword

After you've done all you can to prevent someone from stealing from you, you still need to monitor the use of your images to try to catch anyone who takes your work without permission.

A number of tools are available to help you spot illegal use of your images and/or creative product. Here are a few:

Google (google.com/alerts). You can easily set up a Google Alert to email you when anyone uses a phrase that could be associated with your work. Writers can set up alerts for article titles or key phrases from their books. Artists could enter the names of paintings. And definitely set up an alert for your own name, in case anyone is selling copies of your work without your permission. The service is free and may help you catch some copycats.

Copyscape (copyscape.com). Used primarily for text searches, Copyscape compares words on the pages of your website with words on other websites to try to spot plagiarism. You can use this to find other crafters who have copied your instructions, material descriptions, or the work itself.

TinEye (tineye.com). What Copyscape does for words, TinEye does for images. It lets you search for unauthorized uses of your images, and it works even if the image has been cropped or modified. It's as easy as clicking on your image and then searching to see where else it appears. Learn how to use it at tineye.com/about.

TinEye is simple to use and extremely effective at spotting copied images.

You also can do some simple sleuthing on your own. Browse Etsy a few times a month, searching for items described a lot like yours are. Look for photos of pieces that are blatant copies of your creations. And keep an eye out for copies of your friends' work, too. If everyone works together, a lot more criminals will be caught.

CRAFTY TOOLS

The best source of information about U.S. copyright law is an attorney who specializes in intellectual property and copyright. However, before you start paying big bucks for advice, check through the free information at copyright.gov.

What to Do When You've Been Copied

If you think your work may have been copied, the first thing you should do is talk to an attorney about the situation to discuss your next move. He or she may recommend you contact the offending seller and ask them to remove the copies from his or her Etsy store, or wherever you have found it.

Notifying the Seller

When you contact the seller who appears to be passing off your work as his or her own, be aware that you're officially accusing them of stealing. The seller can then sue you for defamation and damages due to your accusations. So you need to be very careful.

In your letter or email, remain professional and explain the facts as you see them:

- You are the creator of the puppy drawing the seller has emblazoned on hats, shirts, and bumper stickers.

- You have registered the copyright for the image (assuming you have).

- The seller is violating your copyright, as the creator of the drawing.

- You demand the seller immediately remove all items with your image on it from his or her online store and return to you any revenue generated from the sale of that puppy merchandise.

- Copyright violations carry with them statutory damages of $150,000 per incident, plus your attorneys' fees.

Give the offender a deadline by which to comply, and send your letter, if you're not emailing, via certified mail.

Some sellers who realize they've been caught will pull the merchandise immediately. A small percentage who were well aware they were stealing your work will ignore your letter completely, so you need to remain vigilant in monitoring the situation.

Reporting Theft to Etsy

You can also ask for Etsy's support in preventing additional products from being sold on Etsy by copycat sellers. To get Etsy involved, you need to write to the site's legal team and include the following, per Etsy:

> A physical or electronic signature of a person authorized to act on behalf of the owner of the copyright or intellectual property right that has been allegedly infringed upon (by fax or regular mail—not by email, except by prior agreement);

> Identification in sufficient detail of the material being infringed upon (for an allegation of a patent infringement, please provide a patent number);

> Identification of the material that is claimed to be infringing upon the intellectual property. Include information regarding the location of the infringing material with sufficient detail so that Etsy is capable of finding and verifying its existence (for listings, please provide item numbers);

> Contact information about the notifier including the name of the intellectual property owner, the name and title of the person contacting Etsy on the owner's behalf, the address, telephone number and, if available, e-mail address;

> A statement that the notifier has a good faith belief that the material is not authorized by the intellectual property or copyright owner, its agent, or the law; and

> A statement made under penalty of perjury that the information provided is accurate and the notifying party is authorized to make the complaint on behalf of the intellectual property or copyright owner.

Send the notification to:

> Etsy, Inc.
> Attn: Legal Department
> 55 Washington Street, Suite 512
> Brooklyn, NY 11201
> USA
> Fax: 718-732-2613
> Email: legal@etsy.com

Once Etsy has received your infringement notification, it may choose to remove the listing in question and notify the seller of its actions. If the seller is found to have a pattern of copyright violations, Etsy can also decide to ban them from the site.

That seller also has rights, however, and if they do not believe their listing infringes on a copyright—yours or anyone else's—they can send a counternotice. Essentially, it's their response to your claim, providing their side of the story. (If you are ever served with such a claim, this is how you need to respond.)

To issue a counternotice, send a letter to the Etsy legal department (same 55 Washington Street, Suite 512 address) and include the following information, per Etsy:

> Your physical or electronic signature (by fax or regular mail—not by email, except by prior agreement);

> Identification of the material that has been removed or to which access has been disabled and the location at which the material appeared before it was removed or disabled;

> A statement, under penalty of perjury, that the you have a good faith belief that the material was removed or disabled as a result of mistake or misidentification of the material;

> Your name, address, telephone number, and, if available, e-mail address and a statement that you consent to the jurisdiction of the Federal Court for the judicial district in which the Member's address is located, or if your address is located outside the United States, for any judicial district in which Etsy is located, and that you will accept service of process from the person who provided notification under subsection (c)(1)(c) or an agent of such person.

After Etsy receives your counternotice, it then can either reverse the decision to remove the listing or wait to see if the seller files a formal legal action against the copycat. At that point, it's up to the courts to decide who's in the right.

Keep in mind that any lawsuit will be costly, even if you're in the right. And if you win, you still might not recoup your legal expenses. So choose your battles wisely. Some Etsy sellers have pursued clear cases of copying and had to back off because the accused was a corporation with far greater resources. Just fighting the case can cost tens of thousands of dollars, which corporations often have and you may not.

The good news is that Etsy's growth means greater opportunities for you every day. Sure, copycats exist in every industry. That's a given. But don't focus so much on them. Instead, focus on the millions of buyers hunting for something special on Etsy. Just by being there, you've created opportunities to make serious money. For many Etsy sellers, the site has become a springboard for even bigger opportunities.

The Least You Need to Know

- Many types of creative works are protected by copyright, but not everything is protected. Be sure you document any creative thought in writing or by recording.
- You run the risk of your work being copyrighted the moment you show it to another person. Often the rewards (Etsy sales) outweigh the risks.
- You can make it more difficult for copycats to rip off your images and/or present them as their own by shrink-wrapping or watermarking your images.
- If someone violates your copyright, first seek advice from an intellectual property attorney. You also could demand the violator remove your work from their shop and ask Etsy to back you up.

Setting Up Shop

Now that you know what your target customer wants, it's time to start your business. But first you need to register as an Etsy seller. If you've bought before, becoming a seller simply means upgrading your account. And if you're new to Etsy, don't worry—the process is painless.

As your shop starts to take shape, you'll need to make some decisions about how you want to run it. In Etsy-speak, that means setting business policies. Etsy wants you to think through whether you'll accept returns, for example, or which countries you're willing to ship to.

Getting your ducks in a row, Etsy style, also means deciding which forms of payment you'll accept and when and how you'll ship your items to their new owners. Etsy buyers like to be impressed when they open the box containing their purchase, and it's your job to dazzle them. The more you show you care, about your work and the valued customer who likes it, the more successful you'll be.

Registering Your Seller Account

In This Chapter

- Becoming a buyer first and then a seller
- Establishing your Etsy identity
- Naming your shop
- Creating your shop banner

Setting up a shop on Etsy isn't difficult, but before you can start selling your creations, you need to attend to a few administrative tasks first. It's kind of like setting up a bank account and making a deposit before you can start making withdrawals.

When you register your Etsy account and set up the shell of your shop, you need to do some big-picture thinking about the scope of your business. Think about what you're going to sell and if you'll specialize in a particular product category or keep your focus more general. Then you can get down to listing your products for sale.

In this chapter, I help you think through how you want to set up your Etsy shop. Sure, the process is easy, but because some things are set in stone the first time you do them, you'll want to take a second to consider your goals for your shop and where you might want to take it in the future.

Creating Your Account

The first step in getting an Etsy account is to register. To sign up (it's free), click on the **Register** link at the top left of the Etsy home page, next to the Etsy logo. You can also choose to sign up using your Facebook account. Simply click on the Facebook logo, and your Etsy account will link to your Facebook account. Not only does this speed up your registration, but it also creates a connection that can be good for promotion. Whenever you add a new item in Etsy, it will appear in your Facebook status feed, assuming you enable that option.

Or you can choose to register using your email address and then complete the registration form.

| Buy Sell Registry Community Blogs Mobile Gift Cards | Help |

Etsy   Register   Sign In   Search for items and shops   Search

🛒 Cart

Create an Etsy account and start shopping   Sign In

f Sign Up Using Facebook

It's fast and easy. We'll never post without your permission.

or sign up with your email

First Name [   ]   Your name will be publicly displayed on Etsy. These fields are optional.

Last Name [   ]

○ Female ○ Male ○ Rather not say

Signing up for Etsy is quick and easy.

After you've typed in your first and last name (or not, it's optional), indicated whether you're male or female (or decided to play coy), and entered your email address, it's time to get creative.

CRAFTY TOOLS

Before you automatically enter your personal email address, consider whether it makes sense to set up a business-only email, through Gmail, for example. Having a dedicated business email separate from your personal email is a good way to stay on top of buyer questions and orders.

Your Etsy password needs to be at least six characters long and be something easy for you to remember. You don't want to have to look it up every time you go online. But try to make it a little tricky so hackers won't guess it on the first try. Adding a symbol like @, $, or & is a good way to trip them up, as is including a number somewhere in the password. When you've decided on a password, type it once and then type it again to confirm it.

Then the most important step—choosing an Etsy username. This is the name or phrase that represents you as an individual, not your business. However, if you decide to sell products, as I assume you will be, your username will automatically become your shop name. For that reason, you may want to choose a username related to what you expect to sell rather than your actual name.

You can't change your username later, unless you become a seller, in which case you get one and only opportunity to change it when you select a shop name. So think about it for a minute before typing anything. It needs to be 4 to 20 characters long, using only letters and numbers. You also can't use the word *Etsy* in your username, or anything profane or racist. Many people use their real name or initials, while others opt to go with a descriptive phrase, like "Momto3" or "Sewcrazy." Once you've made your choice, or found a username you like that hasn't already been claimed, type it in.

Then, check the **Sign up for the Etsy Finds newsletter** box (it's useful), read through Etsy's Terms of Use and Privacy Policy to be sure you're okay with their policies, and click the **Register** button.

Confirming Your Registration

Once Etsy receives your registration request, you'll receive a confirmation email. Give it an hour to arrive; if you don't have it by then, check your spam folder to see if it got diverted.

This confirmation email is important. Your account won't be activated until you click on the link Etsy sends you. However, if the link you're sent doesn't work, there's a workaround to manually confirm your account.

Sign in to your account using the email and password you requested and then click the **Resend Email** link at the very top of the Etsy home page, or any page within Etsy. You should then see an option to manually confirm your registration. Type in the confirmation code from the email you received (which had the link that didn't work), and you're all set.

After confirming your account, you'll receive a follow-up email from Etsy letting you know your account is ready for use. You can go to the Etsy home page and sign in using the username and password you selected.

> **CRAFTY TOOLS**
>
> Linking a photo of yourself or an image that represents your shop with your Etsy account is a good idea to build rapport with buyers. Many sellers rotate images of their latest pieces, rather than show a headshot. To add a photo, log in to your account, click **Your Account** in the top-right corner and then click **Public Profile**. Click the **Browse** button to review your image files, and select the one you'd like to feature. The image needs to be 75×75 pixels and square. Click **Save Changes** to make it official. For a video on how to do this, visit etsy.com/help/article/2013.

Becoming an Etsy Seller

Now that you have an Etsy account, you can upgrade it from a buyer account to a seller account fairly easily. After logging in to your account, click the **Sell** button in the top left of the Etsy home page to get started and then click the **Open an Etsy Shop** button.

Choose your preferred language and currency. Because Etsy operates globally, sellers from the United States to Canada to the UK to Germany and beyond can do business in their local language and currency.

Next comes the fun part—picking your shop name.

Choosing Your Shop Name

At this point, it's time to start getting more specific about your Etsy business. Don't rush through this part because you may be stuck with a name that won't suit you or your shop long term. So brainstorm some shop names before typing in the first thing that pops in your head.

What should you think about? I'm glad you asked.

Name After What You're Selling

Whether you're a product generalist or specialist may partly drive what you choose for your shop name. If you're going to make and sell any and all kinds of printed stationery, for example, you're going to select a different name than if you were only selling wedding invitations or baby announcements. Maybe "Stationery Central" versus "Nuptial News" or "Wedded Bliss." Likewise, a studio selling art in various media will have a more general name than an artist who works only in pastel or only in watercolor.

Fortunately, you can change your shop name later if your business changes or you come up with something you like better. But when you change it, you'll lose your reputation and the brand identity you've established up to that point. So try to come up with a shop name that will stick. When you have one, type it in the **Set Shop Name** box and click **Save**.

Set your shop, or business, name, and you're one step closer to becoming an Etsy seller.

Use a Clever Play on Words

You don't have to name your shop after what you're selling. Some of the most memorable shop names are whimsical, humorous, and clever. Clever is easier to remember than dry and boring, whether we're talking movies, meals, or Etsy shop names.

Start your brainstorming process by listing words that describe what you sell. What are synonyms for your product? For example, a hat could also be a *cap*, a *Stetson*, a *bonnet*, a *dome cover*, or probably a dozen other terms. Also think about the benefits people usually associate with what you sell. Hats generally provide protection, warmth, style, and pizzazz. So what combinations can you create linking your product name and a benefit? Throw your name in, too, to see if personalizing the shop name sounds good.

See how many different possibilities you can come up with before settling on one and typing it in the **Set Shop Name** box and clicking **Save**.

Setting Up Your Shop

Once you're past the shop name decision, you're nearly home free. Nearly. Only a few more to-dos are in your way.

Your Shop Title

Your shop title is like a book's subtitle—it tells buyers what you sell. It's a description, a really brief description. Whereas Twitter gives you 140 characters to update your friends, Etsy gives you just 55 characters to summarize what you do for buyers. That's 55 letters, numbers, spaces, and symbols; for comparison, you've just read nearly 50 characters in the first part of this sentence.

To add to or edit your Shop Title after you've completed the registration process, go to **Your Shop** in the top-right corner of and click **Info & Appearance** on the drop-down menu. Type your summary, and click **Save**.

Not all Etsy sellers take the time to type up a Shop Title, and they're missing an opportunity to promote their work. Google pays attention to these descriptions and features them in any search results. So someone who searches for your type of product will be given your shop name and title, if you have one. Mine would read "Thriftcycling" and then "Wool and cashmere sweaters for sewing and crafting," which is my Shop Title. Without the Shop Title, you'd probably have no idea what I sell. It's worth a few minutes to come up with a brief description.

CRAFTY TOOLS

The need for brevity in your Shop Title is a strong case for strategic use of keywords. Keywords and phrases are what buyers use to find you—and Google loves them. To learn more about keywords, check out the Etsy Guide to SEO at etsy.com/blog/en/2009/etsy-guide-to-seo.

Your Banner

Next up is creating the banner that runs across the top of your shop. Etsy controls 99 percent of the look and feel of its site, including what shop layouts look like. There's very little you can change in terms of how your products and information are presented to buyers, but you can express your shop's personality and brand identity with your shop's banner.

MILESTONE
DECAL
ART LLC

MilestoneDecalArt
Artisanal Dinnerware, Tile Murals and Gifts Made in NY

♥ Favorite   Like 123

Welcome to our shop! Check out our SHOP SECTIONS on the left sidebar to help you find what you seek!

Milestone Decal Art designs and creates original and personalized porcelain dinnerware, giftware and serving... read more

Erika Boetsch of MilestoneDecalArt created a logo for the back stamp of her company's china, which she then repeated in her Etsy banner.
(© 2012 Milestone Decal Art LLC)

I talk more about what to put in your banner in the upcoming "Designing Your Banner" section.

Your Shop Announcement

Shop announcements are messages that appear at the top of your shop, under the banner, to catch a buyer's attention and alert them to important information about your shop. This is one way to communicate to buyers when you're going to be on a 2-week vacation and unable to ship any purchases, for example, or if you're holding a 25 percent sale this weekend. Include in this section information buyers should have before they make a purchase decision.

Keep in mind that the first 160 characters of the shop announcement becomes the Google snippet that appears when people search for your shop. Because it's so important to Google, it can significantly impact where you appear in search results. To make the best use of it, be sure it tells searchers what you sell or specialize in, rather than that you're on vacation. Knowing you're not in still doesn't tell them anything about your shop. For more information about the important of search engine optimization and shop announcements, watch this handy Etsy video: etsy. com/blog/en/2009/etsy-guide-to-seo.

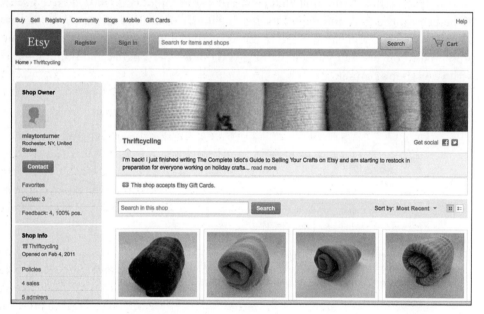

A shop announcement is easy to add and easy to update, so you can write and update them on the fly.

To add a new shop announcement or to change one you previously wrote, go to **Your Shop** and then **Info & Appearance**. After you've typed your announcement, click the **Save Changes** button at the bottom of the page.

Selecting Your Payment Method

At this point, you can actually skip ahead and list something for sale if you like. (See Chapter 10 for detailed step-by-step instructions on the listing process.) However, you may want to continue setting up your shop, including deciding how you'd like to be paid. To do this, click the **Get Paid** tab, and click **Additional payment methods**.

Here are your options; check the boxes beside the methods of payment you'd like to accept:

Direct checkout. A new payment option as of June 2012, U.S.-based sellers can now opt to allow buyers to pay with their Visa, MasterCard, American Express, or Discover credit card directly, rather than through PayPal. The cost for each transaction is 3 percent of the sale plus 25¢, which you pay, just as you do with PayPal. To sign up for direct checkout, click the **Sign Me Up** button. When you make a sale, the proceeds are then deposited in your bank account directly.

PayPal. This is the current standard for online retail payments, so if you don't yet have a PayPal account, it's time you got one. It will take a couple days for PayPal to verify your account, so start that process right away. Most buyers have PayPal accounts and are comfortable using this system. If you already have a PayPal account, check the **PayPal** box and enter your PayPal-associated email address in the **Email** box.

Money order or personal check. To accept money orders and checks, check the boxes beside these options and enter your mailing address. Although few sellers accept personal checks as payment, because of the extra time involved in waiting for the check and for the money to clear, you can opt to allow buyers to pay this way.

Other. U.S. sellers can also choose to accept payment via bank transfer, which may be more convenient for some customers. If you offer buyers this option, you'll need to type in your bank routing number and bank account number for buyers to see when they make a purchase. You'll also want to check with your bank about the cost for such transactions.

Click the **Save** button when you're finished with this page.

Next click the **Billing** tab because it's time to add a credit card number. You'll need a credit card or a debit card with a credit card logo to become a seller. This information is kept on file so you can pay your bill for Etsy fees. It's also kept in case a buyer requests a refund and you don't have enough money in your Shop Payment Account, which is usually PayPal. It's just a backup. After you've entered your information, click **Validate Card**.

All that's left is to click the **Open Shop** button. Now it's time to celebrate. You're officially open for business!

CRAFTY TOOLS

In October 2012, Etsy introduced Etsy gift cards for shoppers to buy and give (or keep for themselves). What this means for you as a seller is that there's another form of payment for you to consider accepting. If you agree to accept Etsy gift cards, you first have to agree to sign up to accept Direct Checkout. After that, the payment by gift card option will appear to buyers and you'll receive money in your Direct Checkout bank account when you receive payment by gift card.

Designing Your Banner

Back to your shop banner. Your 760×100-pixel banner is the only real estate on your shop you can alter, and it provides you with a great opportunity to show your shop's personality. Many shops combine a logo with a background graphic, but you may have to hire a pro to do that for you if you're not adept at Adobe Photoshop. (It's one of the few programs that enables you to overlay text on an image.) However, if you're interested in giving it a shot, Etsy has a great tutorial on creating your own banner at etsy.com/blog/en/2007/skill-share-making-a-banner.

CRAFTY TOOLS

Fiverr (fiverr.com) is a great resource for inexpensive graphic design, where service providers charge just $5 to complete tasks for you. One Fiverr pro will create an Etsy banner and post it to their 3,400 Facebook friends for a five spot. Unless you're a designer, this could be a time-consuming task for you to do on your own.

Your banner should feature an image that suggests what you sell, or the style in which you work or that you emulate. (More on that in the next section.) The same goes for your text—it should help convey your shop's purpose and style.

Choosing a Background Image

There are many potential sources of background images for your banner. You can buy one from a stock photo site such as iStockphoto (istockphoto.com), Shutterstock (shutterstock.com), or Getty Images (gettyimages.com). You'll pay a few bucks for permission to use photos from these sites, but the quality is high and you can be assured your use is permitted if you follow the site's guidelines.

You also can search for royalty-free images on sites like Stock.XCHNG (sxc.hu), FreeDigitalPhotos.net, or Fotosearch (fotosearch.com). Royalty-free images do not require any payment in exchange for use, although some do require you give a photo credit.

 WATCH OUT!

Be sure you have permission to use any image that isn't your own in your Etsy banner. If you buy it or receive permission directly, you're in the clear. But don't just copy an image from a website you like or from a Google image search—those are copyright-protected and you can be sued and fined. Stick with reputable stock image sites.

Of course, you can take your own photo or create an illustration. Those images are yours. And if you've decided to showcase some of your works, this may be the best approach to take.

Selecting a Banner Font

Most sellers feature their shop name in large text over top of an image. And as with images, a huge selection of fonts is available to choose from. Your computer probably came with a long list of fonts you have permission to use, so start by testing out what you already have. If you don't like any from your word processing system, you can also buy CDs with additional typefaces on them or download fonts from free font websites.

Once you've created your banner, added your shop name or other text, and saved the file as a .jpg, .gif, or .png file, you can upload it to your shop. To do so, go to **Your Shop, Info & Appearance**, and scroll to the section dealing with your banner. Using the **Browse** button, find the banner file on your computer, and click **Save**. Voilà! Your banner should now appear on your shop.

The Least You Need to Know

- Once you establish your Etsy account as a buyer, you can immediately upgrade by registering a credit card for billing.
- Your username is the name you'll use as the shop owner. Your shop name is the name of your business on Etsy.
- Most online retailers prefer PayPal or some other payment system, rather than waiting for checks in the mail, although the latter is an option, too.
- Shop announcements are a great way to catch the eye of a buyer with a time-sensitive offer or promotion.
- The only area you can customize to indicate your Etsy shop's style and aesthetic is your banner.

Setting Your Shop Policies

In This Chapter

- Offering payment options
- To refund or not to refund?
- Providing a privacy policy
- Setting a shipping timetable
- Staying in touch with your customers

Buyers will visit your Etsy shop because of your attractive products, but their decision to buy from you depends, in part, on your business policies. If they don't see that you accept returns or that you ship within a certain amount of time, it's likely they'll keep looking, but at someone else's shop.

Etsy shoppers want to be reassured that if something goes wrong with the transaction—the product doesn't arrive, it doesn't arrive in one piece, it isn't what they expected, or some other problem you can't anticipate—that you'll be fair in your dealings with them. For most buyers, that means a willingness to accept returns in sellable shape within a reasonable amount of time and that you'll responsibility if the product is defective or isn't what they expected. The place to show how accommodating you are is in your shop policies.

In this chapter, you learn about setting your own shop policies to ensure you're attracting buyers, rather than scaring them off. How you handle returns and refunds, how quickly you ship items to buyers, what kinds of payments you accept—these are all part of your shop policies, which you'll want to state loud and clear up front. You have many things to consider, but you'll have a clearer idea of what you want your policies to be after the next few pages.

Your Welcome Message

To find where you type your shop policies for all to see, go to **Your Account** and **Info & Appearance**, which will bring up several tabs, including **Shop Policies**. Click on that to get a page with several fields to be filled in related to your policies.

Although not exactly a policy, the first section to be completed is your welcome message. Your welcome message is really just an introduction to your shop and the chance for you to share your philosophy, technique, design aesthetic, and general excitement for your craft. Give potential buyers a sense of who you are and what they're going to find in your shop.

Your Payment Policy

Next, tell buyers what your payment terms are. What forms of payment do you accept? You already established your methods of payment when you set up your shop, but this is a chance to alert shoppers before they put anything in their shopping cart.

PayPal is the standard form of payment on Etsy, and it allows you to receive funds for a purchase immediately. The only downside is that PayPal takes a small fee for the service, and as a result, some buyers don't like to use it. Before you offer it, be sure you have an account set up at PayPal.com.

Buyers' reluctance to use PayPal is why some sellers now also accept direct checkout, which enables buyers to pay using their credit card, without going through PayPal. Like PayPal, you have to set up an account in order to give shoppers this option. Go to **Your Account** and visit the **Payment Methods** page to complete the three-step sign-up process.

You can also allow buyers to pay the old-fashioned way, using personal checks and money orders. Shoppers uncomfortable with sharing their financial information online prefer this method. The disadvantage for you is that if you accept checks and money orders, you'll end up waiting more than a week to receive payment and then confirm that the money is in your account before you can ship the item to the buyer. During that time, your item is not listed for sale, so if your buyer ends up not paying, or sending a bad check, your product will have been off the market for several days. If you have a decent-size inventory, that may not be a big deal, but if you have a smaller shop, it might make a difference to you.

WATCH OUT!

If a buyer asks you to mail their purchase to a different address than what's shown on their PayPal account, don't do it. PayPal won't protect you if you ship to an unconfirmed address, and the buyer can then claim they didn't receive what they bought (because you mailed to a different address). Protect yourself by only shipping after you've been paid, to the address confirmed by PayPal.

Your Return Policy

Etsy sets no hard-and-fast rules regarding what your return policy should be. So although you could decide not to accept returns at all—it is your decision—it's really in your best interests to be flexible.

Put yourself in your buyers' shoes. How comfortable would you feel buying from a shop where everything is a final sale? Probably a little wary, especially if you've never bought anything from that shop before. A better choice is to allow returns, but under certain conditions.

How Much Time Allowed?

The amount of time a customer is permitted to hold on to a purchase before returning it varies widely on Etsy. Each seller makes his or her own policies. Some want products back within 1 week, others say 2 weeks, and some allow 30 days. You need to balance what will make buyers more comfortable—meaning, more time to consider whether the item really meets their needs—and how disruptive returns are to your business. You want to know as soon as possible if someone is sending something back.

Requiring that returns be made in less than 7 days is unreasonable because few buyers will be able to receive their mail, open the package, make a decision, and get it back in the mail to you to arrive within a week. On the other hand, allowing your buyers more than 30 days to return a purchase opens the door to the possibility they'll use it and then send it back. It's not likely, but the more time you give, the higher the chances that item will not be in brand-new condition when you get it back.

Providing Refunds

Etsy asks sellers to be fair with respect to refunds. This means offering a replacement item or a refund of the full purchase price if the item arrives damaged.

CRAFTY TOOLS

To prevent financial loss due to items damaged during shipping, be sure to purchase insurance from the shipper. Then, if a shipment is damaged, you can refund the buyer and still be reimbursed for your costs.

If a buyer reports that an item hasn't arrived and you can't confirm that it got there, it would seem only fair that you refund the buyer's purchase price. Avoiding this scenario is one reason most shippers buy proof of delivery. It's often free or inexpensive, depending on which shipper you use, and you can track the shipment and receive notification of its arrival. It's harder for buyers to claim nondelivery when the shipper confirms the package arrived.

It gets trickier when a buyer requests a refund because the color of the necklace isn't what they expected, or the size of the skirt is too big or too small. Is that your fault? Probably not, but you do want to maintain positive seller ratings, so it's in your best interest to try to make the customer happy. So if they agree to return the item, you should probably refund their money. It's up to you, but wouldn't you want your money back if you returned an item?

If that's how you decide you'll handle situations when the customer isn't happy, you may opt to write your policy fairly loosely—that any item can be returned for a full refund if received within a certain number of days. You'll need to determine what you think is fair. Looking at other Etsy sellers' policies is a good way to decide what makes sense for you.

Noting Exceptions

If you agree to accept returns for a full refund, except in some situations, you need to spell out those exceptions in advance. For example, if you sell perishables, such as homemade jams and jellies, you may decide not to accept returns after a certain amount of time, in case the product has gone bad. Or maybe you don't want to take it back at all, in case the product has been opened and can't be resold.

It would seem fair not to accept returns of items that were damaged by the buyer, although this would be hard to prove. You could also refuse returns on items that weren't in sellable condition, such as if the buyer wore the item a few times.

Keep in mind that you can update your policies at a moment's notice within Your Account, so don't be nervous about being stuck forever with the same return policy. You can revise it if you find buyers taking advantage of you.

Your Privacy Policies

Etsy has its own privacy policy. Find it by clicking **Help** on the home page, clicking **Site Policies** on the bottom-right side of the Help page, and clicking **Privacy** in the left column.

Etsy's policy states that the company will not share or sell members' and buyers' personal information with third parties. However, Etsy sellers can set their own policies for their shops, which is why you need to communicate your privacy policies to buyers.

Do You Share Customer Information?

When someone buys from you, what do you do with that information? Or what might you do with it in the future? Consumers are increasingly wary of sharing any personal information on websites for fear that their name, address, phone number, email address, and shopping data might be shared with other companies. Most consumers do not want this and would like to receive assurance from you that if they do business with you, you won't turn around and sell their name and contact information to Publishers Clearinghouse or anywhere else. That's where your own privacy policy comes in.

If you intend to create a buyer mailing list and keep in touch with your customers, let them know that. Or at a minimum, be sure they can opt out of the mailings at any time. And if you could see yourself trading mailing lists with other Etsy sellers or other companies, or renting your list to outside organizations, you need to be upfront and inform your buyers. It's not recommended that you share your buyers' contact information, but you need to tell them of your plans.

And if, like the majority of websites, you have no intention of ever sharing your customer list with anyone else, tell your buyers that, too. They'll feel better buying from you knowing this upfront. If you change your mind in a couple years, you can update your policy and tell your customers then, but if you aren't doing that now, your privacy policy should be very similar to Etsy's.

Do You Use Customer Info Another Way?

You also need to tell customers if you will keep their information and use it in other ways, such as to keep in touch. As mentioned in the preceding section, some Etsy sellers have a regular email newsletter they use to stay in touch with buyers. If you'll retain customer contact information in order to keep them updated about upcoming products and news they may be interested in, ask for their permission to add them to your email list.

WATCH OUT!

Most people don't appreciate being automatically added to an email list, even if they bought your work. You just won't know until you ask. So do that—invite them to subscribe to your email newsletter and leave it at that.

Your Shipping Policies

You have many possible ways to ship customer packages, so you should tell buyers in your Shop Policies how they should expect to receive their purchase. Do you only use a particular carrier, such as USPS, UPS, or FedEx? Do you promise to ship within a certain number of days of receipt of payment? Do you offer insurance? Will you upgrade the shipping method for an additional fee? Will you combine shipping when several items are ordered at once?

Share these policies and options with buyers so they know what to expect. If you tell them you ship within 48 hours via USPS Priority Mail, they can estimate when to look for it (4 or 5 days later) and not become impatient when their order doesn't arrive the next day. Even better, email them when the package is picked up by UPS or FedEx or when you mail it at the post office. Include a tracking number, too. That way, they can monitor its delivery progress and know exactly when to expect it. Stating your policies upfront also increases the likelihood of receiving positive feedback rather than complaints.

Shipping Internationally

Some Etsy users only sell and ship to buyers within the United States. U.S. shipping is among the most reliable in the world, so you'll generally encounter fewer problems. However, the size of the market outside the United States is several times larger than the domestic one so agreeing to ship internationally is likely to have a very positive impact on your sales. You've just exponentially increased the size of your potential market of buyers!

Choosing to ship internationally doesn't mean you have to ship to every country in the world; you can be selective. Certainly ship to Canada and Mexico, with which we have trade agreements. But you may elect to ship anywhere, as long as there are no trade restrictions. For a list of prohibited exports from the United States, go to cfr. vlex.com/vid/prohibited-exports-sales-countries-19719898.

In your Shipping Policies section, list the countries to which you'll send orders. I also suggest you indicate that the buyer is responsible for confirming you are permitted to sell your products there.

Shipping Prohibited Products

Some countries do not allow certain products to be imported. Unless you do business internationally on a large scale, it's very likely you won't be familiar with the prohibited list for Norway, or South Africa, or New Zealand, for example. But the people who live there—your customers—should know.

So in your policies, make it clear that you will not ship prohibited products to countries that do not allow them and that it's the buyer's responsibility to confirm their purchase is allowable. That way, if you mistakenly mail a handmade hat to Italy and it gets confiscated (because hats may not be imported there), you aren't responsible for refunding the purchase price to your customer.

Dealing with Missing Packages

It's very likely that at some point, one of your shipments will go missing. It may not be your fault, but the end result will be that your customer does not receive the order they paid you for. So what will you do? Refund their money? Say too bad? That's one of the big questions buyers need answered up front, as a measure of how reputable you are.

If you insured the package against loss or damage, you can refund your customer and make a claim with your shipper so you're also compensated for the loss. It costs a little more money, but it's insurance that you won't lose out if your shipment gets lost. And you can reassure potential buyers they won't lose out either.

CRAFTY TOOLS

Paying for insurance on your own, rather than giving buyers the option to get it, reduces your risk. It's your responsibility to get the package to your buyer, and if something goes wrong en route, you may have to issue a refund. In that case, you've not only lost out on a sale, you've lost your inventory, too. To protect yourself, build in the cost of insurance to every shipping charge.

Your Communications

Another gauge of how reputable you are as a business person is the amount of communication you provide to your customers. The more communication, the more helpful you come across as and the more positive your buyers will feel about you. When in doubt, more communication is preferred to less.

When Will Buyers Hear from You?

When setting your business policies, you may also want to let buyers know when they should expect to hear from you. This gives you the opportunity to keep them informed about their purchase and to prove your trustworthiness by keeping promises regarding updates.

Letting customers know when they will hear from you also helps manage their expectations in that regard. If you tell them you send out shipping confirmations within 2 or 3 days of payment, your buyers know to watch for such a communication from you. Likewise, if you promise that orders within the United States will be delivered via Parcel Post within 2 weeks, you help customers understand how you do business.

How Often Will Buyers Hear from You?

Telling your customers when and how often they'll hear from you is another way to reassure them that you're a reputable Etsy seller. For example, you might email customers for some or all of the following reasons:

- To thank them for their order and tell them you're processing it
- To ask questions or get clarification regarding a purchase, especially when you've received a custom order
- To confirm that you've mailed their purchase
- To provide a shipment tracking number
- To follow up after the package has been delivered to be sure they're happy with their purchase
- To offer a free subscription to your customer enewsletter
- To announce special sales or promotional offers

Customers generally appreciate being kept in the loop while they're waiting for a purchase, but after it has arrived, the frequency of your emails should decline.

Establishing clear business policies up front and communicating them on your Etsy shop page demonstrates that you are a professional, builds confidence and trust with your customers, and reduces the amount of customer support you need to provide after the sale. Take a few minutes to fill in yours now.

The Least You Need to Know

- How do you like to be treated by retailers when making a purchase? Use those expectations to guide your own Etsy shop policies.
- Etsy has its own policies, but as a shop owner, you can set your own regarding returns and refunds, shipping speed, privacy, and communication.
- Expanding your Etsy business from domestic to international increases the size of your market but also requires you to know international shipping processes and regulations.
- Tracking shipments after they leave your business protects you should a package get lost. You can refund your buyer, protect your reputation, and get reimbursed.
- The more communication you have with your buyers, the more trustworthy and reputable your buyers will assume you to be.

Choosing a Payment System

In This Chapter

- Offering payment options
- Dealing with paper payments
- Receiving online payments
- Avoiding payment scams

One of the biggest, if not *the* biggest, reason you opened an Etsy shop to sell your crafts is to make money. A few years ago, being paid after a sale meant receiving and accepting a check or money order in the mail. The check took days to arrive and then even more time to clear the bank. Fortunately, today, you have several additional payment options that can allow you to get that money in your account almost instantaneously.

If you're like most online sellers, you prefer to receive payments electronically so you can ship the order to the buyer quickly, knowing you have their money. It's a much more efficient process, with the whole sale and shipment potentially happening in a matter of hours. However, not all buyers feel comfortable paying with a credit or debit card online, and some don't trust PayPal. They want to pay by check or money order. As you set up your payment system, you need to weigh your interest in being paid efficiently with what payment options your buyers want.

In this chapter, you learn about the pros and cons of your various payment options, how to specify how you want to be paid, and how to set that up within your Etsy shop.

Accepting Checks

Until recently, paper checks were the only way consumers could pay their bills if they didn't want to pay cash in person. You wrote the check for the proper amount, placed it in an envelope with the bill, and mailed it off. After the recipient cashed your check—whether it was your electric utility or your nephew—your monthly bank statement confirmed the funds had been deducted.

However, the ease with which bank accounts can be accessed online today means checks are almost obsolete. Many consumers prefer to pay their bills online, directing their credit card company or bank to deduct a bill's amount from their account on a specific date. No check writing; no mailing. Just click Submit and the payment is made in seconds.

As an Etsy seller, accepting checks from buyers might sound like a lot of hassle. You have to wait for the buyer to write the check and mail it, and when you receive it, you need to wait a few days for the money to appear in your bank account. But for some buyers, this is the preferred method of payment, so you should at least consider accepting checks.

The Various Forms of Checks

The most common type of check is the personal variety, which is drawn on a buyer's own bank. When you receive a personal check, you can call the bank and confirm there are sufficient funds available to pay you. Be aware that the buyer may have written several checks against their bank balance, so until your check is presented, you can't really be sure there will be money in the buyer's account to pay you. Don't ship the order until you have cash in your hands or a deposit in your checking account.

> **WATCH OUT!**
>
> Cash checks promptly. Most banks won't cash checks more than 90 days old, and some limit it to 60 days.

If you're not comfortable accepting personal checks as payment, because of the hassle of wondering if they're good or not, you might want to list cashier's checks or money orders as options instead. This allows people who do not have a credit card, or who are not familiar with or comfortable with online purchases, to still do business with you.

Unlike personal checks, where the money remains in the buyer's checking account until you withdraw it when you cash their check, with a money order, the buyer already handed over the cash when he or she purchased the money order. You have more certainty with a money order. It's guaranteed by the issuing bank or agency so you know it won't bounce.

If you do decide to accept money orders, it's still a good idea to check their legitimacy. Counterfeit money orders are in circulation. Either call the bank to confirm funds are in the account on which the check is drawn, or call the issuer of the money order to verify it's legit. Better safe than sorry when money is involved.

The Downside of Accepting Checks

Accepting checks may increase the size of your buyer pool, but only you can decide if the inconvenience of having to take the checks to your bank, deposit them, and wait for them to clear is worth it. You have to decide if having to wait for the check, and wait to learn whether there's actually money in the account to pay for the item purchased, is worth your time.

And then there's the possibility that even after you wait for a check to arrive, it could still bounce when you go to cash it. Incurring a bounced check charge of $20 or more for each bad check you receive, which you may not be able to get back, is another hassle. Meanwhile, during the time you're waiting for the check to arrive, you've marked the item in your shop as sold, and other interested buyers may have come shopping for something similar.

Yet despite these downsides, if you find many of your buyers asking if you'll accept checks, you might want to consider adding it to your accepted forms of payment. At the start, however, you may find it easier to insist on electronic payments.

Online Payment Systems

PayPal is currently the default electronic payment system on Etsy, but you can certainly accept others. Recently, Etsy added direct checkout using a credit card as another means of accepting electronic payments, in addition to personal checks, money orders, and other forms.

Etsy allows you to choose from among five basic forms of payment, although the Other category gives you the freedom to work with virtually any electronic system you want.

A number of other online payment systems are also growing in popularity, including Dwolla, which is great for smaller amounts; Google Checkout; Serve; and WePay.

PayPal

PayPal is one of the largest online payment companies in the world and boasts more than 110 million active accounts. Owned by eBay, PayPal is the preferred way for eBay buyers and sellers to transact business today and has been the preferred payment method at Etsy, too.

More than 110 people worldwide use PayPal to pay for purchases online, as well as to receive payments from others.

Odds are good that shoppers who regularly buy online already have a PayPal account. With money deposited in their PayPal account, or via a link to their checking or savings account, buyers can quickly pay you for their Etsy purchase. What's nice about PayPal is that you can log into your account and immediately see when someone has paid you. You can then transfer those funds into your bank account.

The cost to accept money via PayPal is 2.9 percent of the transaction value plus 30¢. There's no cost to transfer the money to your bank account.

This fee is on top of Etsy's 3.5 percent transaction and 20¢ listing fee. It's deducted directly from the proceeds of the sale, before it's even deposited in your payment account. So for each sale you make that's paid for via PayPal, you receive 97.1 percent of the value, minus an additional 30 cents. Etsy bills you separately for its listing and final value fees.

CRAFTY TOOLS

If you don't already have a PayPal account, it would be a good idea to set one up. At PayPal.com, you'll enter your personal information and then wait a couple days for your information to be verified. During that time, PayPal will deposit a small amount in your bank account. You'll report to PayPal when the money arrives and how much was deposited to prove the account is yours and is active. Then you're all set.

PayPal is the leading online payment system, but it's not the only one, which Etsy seems to realize. Now buyers can use their credit card to pay for purchases, and sellers can accept that money without having to set up a separate merchant account for their business.

Direct Checkout

Direct checkout is the newest payment option on Etsy. With direct checkout, Etsy buyers can pay for their purchases with any major credit card. After their payment is processed, you receive payment in your Shop Payment Account once you mark the item as shipped or 3 days from the sale, whichever comes later. When the money's in your account, you can transfer it to your bank account, just as you would with PayPal, or Etsy will automatically transfer it the following Monday.

There's a fee to use direct checkout, which you, as the seller, pay. It costs 3 percent of the purchase price plus shipping and tax, and a flat 25¢-per-order fee. For smaller-value orders, the cost is right in line with what PayPal charges.

Direct checkout is Etsy's own service, designed to allow buyers to use major credit cards without going through PayPal. Sign up is quick and easy.

Merchant Account

Until Etsy's direct checkout service was introduced, sellers could only accept credit cards from buyers through PayPal, which some sellers didn't like, or by setting up a merchant account with a bank or merchant service. With a merchant account, your business can accept credit cards as payment directly, without going through a third-party service like PayPal or direct checkout.

The upside of taking the time to fill out paperwork and set up a merchant account is that it adds to your business's credibility. In some instances, it also may be less expensive than PayPal or direct checkout. It depends on the merchant account provider you choose.

Most banks can set you up with a merchant account, but check the fees involved; that may not be your best option. Other big merchant account companies include Merchant Warehouse, Flagship Merchant Services, Paysimple, and Intuit Payments, among many others. Be sure you're not being overcharged if you don't process many credit cards each month.

If you sell your crafts at venues other than Etsy, it might be worth the time to set up your own mobile merchant account. Then, at craft fairs or festivals, you can accept credit cards using a swipeable reader attached to your smartphone.

CRAFTY TOOLS

Square (square.com) enables you to accept credit cards remotely using your smartphone. When you sign up for Square, you receive a small phone attachment through which you swipe credit cards and receive payment. You don't need a merchant account to use Square. The fee is 2.75 percent of each swipe.

No matter which route you decide to take with respect to online payments, the key message here is that more customers are going to want to pay electronically than the old-fashioned way, with checks. And you need to think about whether you even want to deal with the hassle checks saddle you with.

Avoiding Scams

Scam artists are everywhere online, including on Etsy. There's no real way you can stop them from trying to take your money, other than recognizing when you're dealing with a shady buyer. Scammers can't take your money without your involvement or permission, so be on alert with every transaction, and when a buyer asks you to bend the rules for them, think twice.

Get Paid First, Ship Second

Above all else, you can protect yourself by holding on to the merchandise until you receive payment. Do not mail buyers their purchase until you have confirmation that the funds are in your account. Otherwise, you run the risk of losing out on the value of your product *plus* the money you thought you were receiving.

Recently, the most common online scam seems to be that a buyer commits to a purchase but then asks you to jump through hoops to get their purchase to them. Maybe they want you to ship the item to an address different from their confirmed PayPal address, or they want to make a bank transfer and need all sorts of personal information from you in order to effect the transaction. Don't do it! Don't give them that option, and certainly don't share any personal information with anyone.

> **WATCH OUT!**
> Scammers can also report that they never received their purchase and request a refund. Be sure you have proof of mailing and, preferably, proof of delivery, too. Without them, you may be out some money if your buyer claims not to have received the package.

Monitor Your Accounts

It's not always easy to tell when you're dealing with a shady character. And if a transaction seems to be going smoothly, you might have no reason to question the legitimacy of your buyer. But do keep a close watch on your bank account, your PayPal account, and your Etsy Shop Payment Account. Watch your balances like a hawk.

If a scammer is going to try to renege on a deal or request a refund, the notice of their request will likely come through their method of payment. To fight any refund requests, you'll need to have all your paperwork in order, including proof you mailed the item. Most scammers will request a refund based on a claim that they didn't receive an item or it was damaged. To protect yourself, always get delivery confirmation and insurance. That way, even if the scammer wins and gets their money back, your insurance claim will cover all your costs.

Keep Detailed Records

Most importantly, keep track of each and every transaction—in particular when you shipped it, which carrier you used, and the delivery confirmation code for tracking the package. You'll need this information if a buyer disputes having received their order.

The good news is that very, very few Etsy buyers are scam artists. The vast majority are people like you and me who love handmade items. They appreciate the skill and workmanship you demonstrate with your crafts and want to support you. Only when there is a legitimate problem will you hear from them with bad news. So it's smart to be organized and prepared in case an issue does come up, but know that such situations are very rare. Most shipments you send out will be received and loved—and followed by positive feedback.

The Least You Need to Know

- Decide what forms of payment you'll accept from buyers. Etsy's default options are PayPal, direct checkout, personal check, money order, and other.
- If you accept checks, you'll have to wait until you receive the physical check and also wait to see if the funds are available before considering the sale complete.
- PayPal is the largest and most commonly used online payment system. Being able to pay for purchases electronically simplifies the process for buyers, which makes them more likely to buy from you.
- Direct checkout acts like a merchant account, allowing you to accept any major credit card. The money is deposited in your Etsy account and then transferred to your bank account.
- Accepting electronic payments is much more efficient, and speeds along the sales process, but it does cost you around 3 percent more, on top of your Etsy fees.
- Beware of scam artists on Etsy. Never ship an order until you've confirmed you've been paid, and keep careful records to prove the item was shipped and the buyer received it.

Developing a Packing and Shipping Strategy

In This Chapter

- Adding pizzazz with your packaging
- Making your products feel like presents
- Safe and secure shipping
- Keeping shipping costs to a minimum

The moment your customer opens the box containing her order from you, you want her reaction to be surprise and delight, not letdown. This is your prime opportunity to make a great first impression by giving your buyer more than she expected. Sure, she's excited to hold her purchase in her hand, but how about throwing in something to push her satisfaction way over the top?

Giving more than your customers expect, either in packaging and presentation or by way of a present, not only increases the odds of getting very positive feedback, but also builds trust and rapport that can lead to more sales from those same customers.

What's a little tricky is giving more than your buyer's order without weighing down your package to the point it costs you extra money to ship it. You want to wow your customer, but you don't want to give up all your profits either. Fortunately, I've collected some tips for great bonuses that won't break the bank.

In this chapter, I share some tips for efficient and effective order packaging that will wow buyers without costing you a lot more in shipping charges.

Perfect Product Presentation

When someone makes a purchase from you, they may be buying for themselves or for someone else—you can't usually tell. It's very possible that your customer is feeling a little nervous about her purchase and whether it will turn out to be a suitable teacher gift or thank you present for a friend. Keeping this in mind, you want to do all you can to impress whomever opens the box containing your piece. That starts with how your product is wrapped and packaged.

Sure, you can simply wrap it in bubble wrap or place it in a sealed plastic bag inside a cardboard box, depending on how delicate or breakable it is, but how will that look when the buyer opens it? *Impressive* is not a word that springs to my mind. *Expected*, *cheap*, and *minimalist* maybe, but not *impressive*.

To really wow the recipient, you need to wrap your product as if it were a present. Who cares if it's not for a particular occasion—how about dressing it up, just because? Sometimes the blandest or least-expensive items can end up looking stunning and worth a lot of money just by taking a few steps to enhance their appearance.

Always Overdeliver

Your buyer has certain expectations about what they've ordered from you. They expect it will reach them in a reasonable amount of time undamaged. They also expect it will look exactly like the photo you showed them on Etsy.

If you can meet all these expectations, your buyer will likely be satisfied with their purchase. But is "satisfied" all you want them to be? That's kind of a low bar, don't you think? Why not aim to surprise and delight your customers by delivering more value than they expected? That's how you win repeat customers.

Here are some ways to enhance the overall appearance of your package:

- Add a handmade gift tag or hang tag
- Place it in a gift box
- Surround it with tissue paper
- Put it in a cellophane bag
- Top it with a silk flower or decoration
- Print a little how-to booklet to accompany the item

- Wrap a fabric ribbon around it, with a bow

- Enclose a handmade card with a greeting, or even a business card with your Etsy shop info and a personalized, handwritten note on the back (Customers like to be reminded that a live person made what they bought.)

- Put it inside a piece of origami you've made

- Put it inside a reusable shopping bag

Anything you do above and beyond mailing a customer's order to them promptly will likely put a smile on their face, but if you can make that package even more attractive, they'll really be pleased and surprised. That's overdelivering.

CRAFTY TOOLS

You can also offer gift wrapping as a service to customers for an additional fee. Mention it in your item listing, shop profile, and shop announcement, and let buyers know what the extra charge is. Then just update the shipping charge to reflect this additional service.

The Importance of Bonuses

Another way to provide more than customers expect is by enclosing a freebie or bonus with each order. A true bonus is something you enclose with a shipped order that you hadn't previously mentioned or advertised. Its goal is to increase your buyer's perceived value of the purchase.

Bonuses don't have to be expensive—or even handmade, for that matter. They just need to be related in some way to what your customer has bought or you think they'll appreciate.

Here are some examples of bonuses:

- A new pacifier included with a baby blanket

- A package of nails and hook included with a framed drawing

- An extra bead or charm included with a charm bracelet

- An extra ink cartridge included with a handmade wooden pen

- A matching hair band included with a little girl's skirt

- Wine glass tags included with hand-blown champagne flutes

- A nice cigar included with a humidor

- A lip balm included with a body lotion or soap

- A mini version of a hand-sewn stuffed animal included with the original

- A small jar of silver polish included with new silver jewelry

- Dog treats included with a dog bed or leash

- Candles included with candle holders

- If you can't think of anything that exactly complements an order, candy is always welcome—just don't mail a box of chocolates during the summer

Think about how your customer will use your product and brainstorm potential low-cost and lightweight freebies. Is there a complementary item you can buy inexpensively? Or something you can easily make when finishing the order?

You don't have to go overboard and make a bonus that's anywhere close in value to the customer's purchase, but if you can save them a trip to the store to buy something they'll need in order to use their new purchase, you've done them a big favor. Think batteries for toys at Christmas—you want to anticipate what your customers will need to have in order to immediately try out what you've made for them.

WATCH OUT!

Some sellers enclose a coupon for a percentage off the customer's next purchase as a freebie, but it's not really an added bonus. It's more of an incentive to buy more. It's fine to include a coupon, but it won't elicit the same type of appreciation a true bonus will.

Shipping Do's and Don'ts

As you're packing up a customer's order and bonus gift, keep in mind how you'll ship it. The larger the box or padded envelope needed, the higher the cost. And the heavier the box, the higher the cost. So do what you can to minimize added weight as you prep each shipment.

Protection Is Job One

Although you want to wow your customer when they open your package, your biggest concern should be ensuring that it arrives in good condition. Nothing blows a sale, and causes extra paperwork for you, than having an order arrive broken or damaged. Then you have to refund the buyer's payment and make a claim with your shipping carrier.

Breakage happens every once in a while, no matter how hard you try to prevent it, but do your best to wrap and protect your pieces so the risk of breakage is minimal.

FedEx recommends a four-step process to prepare your item for shipment:

1. Using bubble wrap, cushion your product by wrapping it several times around and sealing it with packing tape.

2. Place your wrapped item in a box, and surround it with packaging peanuts or popcorn to prevent the item from shifting while en route. If it's an especially fragile piece, consider placing it in a box with peanuts and then placing that box in an even bigger box for added cushioning.

3. Seal the box with packing tape across the top, the bottom, and along the edges, to provide closure and support.

4. Label the box on the outside as well as on the inside. A packing slip inside the box is a good idea in case the outside label comes off during shipment.

Most shipping carriers—such as USPS, UPS, FedEx, and others—have guidelines for shipping you need to follow in order to qualify for reimbursement if an order is damaged. You may want to read those on each carrier's website to be sure you're meeting their minimum guidelines in case you run into a problem. It would be frustrating to have an order damaged, have to reimburse your customer, and then not be able to get any money back for the shipment or damage.

WATCH OUT!

As part of the listing process, you had to quote a cost to ship your item. It's always a good idea to pack a product for shipping early, so you can get an accurate weight and associated cost for the product, packing, and box. If you don't weigh the whole box, you may end up undercharging your customers and eating the extra cost yourself.

Small Is the New Big

With shipments billed based on physical size and weight, it's in your best interest to make your products as compact as possible. Don't use a 12×10×15-inch box if a smaller one will do. You'll pay more for the larger one because it takes up more space on the truck.

If you have something that can be folded or wrapped tightly, such as clothing, do that and consider mailing it in a padded envelope. With flat items, such as prints or stationery, look to thick, flat envelopes for shipment.

The smaller the package, the lower the cost, so do what you can to keep your shipments compact and as small as possible without risking damage to your creation.

Minimizing Your Shipping Costs

Although you might not realize it, there's a cost to ship items above and beyond what you pay the U.S. Postal Service, UPS, or FedEx.

To prepare your crafty products for mailing, you need boxes or bags, packing tape, bubble wrap, packing peanuts, address labels, even plastic bags. These items might not be overly expensive, but there is a cost to each of these shipping tools, and you'll want to keep those numbers as low as possible. The more you spend on shipping supplies, the less profit you enjoy.

> **CRAFTY TOOLS**
>
> The U.S. Postal Service will send you Priority or Express envelopes from their website, USPS.gov—for free. This is the biggest benefit of using Priority service—you don't have to pay anything for the shipping cartons and envelopes.

Using Lightweight Materials

Because the cost of your shipments is calculated based on weight and size, choose supplies that are light as a feather. Sure, gravel will help stabilize a candle or a plant inside your shipping box, but it will also likely double the shipping cost because of its weight.

Here are some of the best lightweight supplies:

- Plastic bags filled with air, like what Amazon uses

- Plastic peanuts, preferably reused from another shipment

- Bubble wrap

- Plain newsprint, without printing on it

- Cardboard stabilizers to hold items in place, without the need for additional stuffing around it

Always look for a lighter-weight alternative when packing a box.

CRAFTY TOOLS

After you've packed your box, you can either drop it off at a post office, or you can schedule a pick-up for no additional charge if you're using Priority or Express mail service from the U.S. Postal Service.

Finding Low-Cost Supplies

You can certainly go out to your local office supply store to stock up on brand-new shipping supplies, but you'll also pay top dollar. To keep your supply costs to a minimum and maximize your profits, take advantage of these opportunities:

- Ask liquor stores for leftover boxes—they're usually extremely sturdy because of the need to keep bottles from breaking. And they're free.

- Reuse any packing materials, such as peanuts, you receive when you order through the mail.

- Watch for sales and promotional offers at office supply stores. Many have rebate offers that will net you pens, labels, and other supplies for free.

- Dollar stores often sell padded envelopes, packing tape, scissors, and pens for $1. That's a good deal.

- Ship orders via Priority Mail so you can take advantage of the free shipping supplies the U.S. Postal Service provides. You can order what you need online or pick them up at your local post office.

To be sure you're paying the absolute lowest shipping rate, ask your carrier about any discounts you may be entitled to. FedEx, for example, offers Etsy sellers discounts of up to 21 percent, plus an additional 5 percent when they create and print shipping labels at FedEx.com. Generally, packages under 2 pounds cost the least at the USPS, but for packages weighing more than 2 pounds, UPS is an attractive alternative. Check to be sure that's the case with your particular boxes, however.

WATCH OUT!

It's fine to save money on shipping and packing supplies, but never skimp when it comes to insuring your packages. Yes, it may cost an extra dollar, but it gives you peace of mind that if anything goes awry en route, your customer and you will be covered. They'll get their money back, and so will you.

The Least You Need to Know

- Take time to wrap up your package to surprise and delight your customer when she opens the box. The more you exceed her expectations, the better your chances she'll be a repeat customer.

- Bonus gifts are becoming common practice on Etsy. Include a little extra something, something small that complements the purchase, to brighten your customer's day.

- Keeping your product safe and secure en route is essential. Wrap it in bubble wrap and place it in a box surrounded by packing peanuts to prevent any shipping damage.

- You can order free Priority Mail supplies from the U.S. Postal Service. Although the shipping cost is a little higher, you eliminate the need to pay for boxes.

- With a little effort, you can amass a large supply of low- and no-cost scissors, tape, boxes, stickers, and other shipping supplies.

Selling 101

Now comes the fun part—prepping and listing your works of art for sale. The listing process itself is just a series of questions—nothing to worry about—but before you start to write your listing, be sure you've thought through your pricing strategy. Have you looked to see what other Etsy sellers are charging for similar items? Or at least items in your category, whether that's clothing or dried flowers or ceramic vases? Before you set your prices, confirm that they're high enough to generate a profit but not so high no one will buy them.

How you describe your work is also important. Telling a story about your inspiration for your work and the artistic process can really set you apart. And good, crisp photos are essential. Once you understand what it takes to get a top-notch Etsy photo, you'll be good to go.

As the money starts rolling in, you'll want to set up some processes for tracking your sales and monitoring your expenses. You want to be sure you're profitable on each item.

Selling is the culmination of all your work setting up your Etsy store, creating your beautiful pieces, and presenting them to the world. Get ready for some fun!

Pricing Your Work

In This Chapter

- Estimating your production costs
- Taking your time into account
- Determining the going rate
- Positioning your work properly
- Achieving your goal—profitability

Surprisingly, the key to your success on Etsy has less to do with the quality of your crafts than with the price you ask customers to pay. Price your items too high and buyers will look elsewhere for a better deal. Price them too low and you may sell a bunch but make too little money for all your efforts.

The trick to pricing your crafts effectively is part art and part science. Yes, you need to take into account what it costs you to make each of your pieces, but how much you tack on as profit can vary greatly. And this, too, varies by season, current demand, fashion trends, and the state of the economy, to name a few factors.

To ensure you're pricing your crafts high enough to generate a profit and to be taken seriously, but low enough not to seriously limit your market to the top earning 1 percent of the population, you'll want to get a handle on all your costs and then study your market—both buyers and sellers. You can also experiment; no one ever said your original price can't change. But before you start raising and lowering your prices, be sure you've accounted for all your expenses and understand what your target market is used to paying for similar products on Etsy.

When you do settle on the price that works best for you and your customers, you may be surprised at how quickly your Etsy sales ramp up.

In this chapter, you get tips for controlling costs to be sure you're making money on every craft you create and list on Etsy.

Setting Etsy Sales Goals

If you aren't already selling on Etsy, or if you've been selling only casually, and you want to set some sales goals, you have a few ways to approach it. Going through this process helps you understand how many pieces you need to sell in a month or year to hit your desired income level, which may or may not be possible. This is a reality check.

One of the simplest ways is to decide how much you'd like to make in the next year. This is your gross sales target, meaning your total sales.

> Annual sales target = $_____

To break that down into how much you need to make per month, divide your annual sales goal by 12 months.

> Monthly sales target = annual sales target ÷ 12 = $_____ per month

You can then further break that down into how many products you need to sell per month in order to hit your goal. To see that, take your monthly sales target, for example, and divide by the average price you expect to charge for your pieces. That will tell you how many products per month you need to sell at that price to hit your annual goal.

> Monthly sales goal ÷ average sales price = number of units you need to sell per month to make your income goal

Keep in mind, however, that it may take a while to start selling consistently on Etsy. You need buyers to find you, which can take some time. Also, the more products you put up for sale, the better your odds of hitting your sales target. Don't list 20 items for sale if you need to sell all 20 to reach your goal. It would be better to list 40, to give buyers more of a selection.

> **WATCH OUT!**
>
> Putting a low price tag on your work will certainly attract bargain hunters, but you might make it difficult to raise your prices later. You'll position your products as less expensive, and you'll attract price-sensitive shoppers, which will limit your profits. Pricing your pieces even a tad higher increases your profits and indicates your work is worth more.

Calculating Your Costs

You might have an idea of what you'd like to sell your products for price-wise, but before you can accurately price them, you need to be sure you are *at least* covering all your costs. And the only way to know that is if you break down your costs and add up all your expenses.

Here are the major categories to take into account:

Raw materials. This is the stuff you use to create your art or your crafts. Fabric, paint, wood, and paper are all raw materials, as are thread, glue, and brushes. Make a list of all the components of your work, and note what you paid for them.

Manufacturing cost. If your product requires processing by someone else, such as sewing or even using equipment you don't own, and there's a fee for that work, that's a cost you need to take into account.

Labor cost. Although you might not realize it, your time has value. Even when you're working in front of the TV or on the deck in the evening, you need to factor in the cost of that time when pricing your products. And if you pay others to help you produce your pieces, you need to add in those expenses, too.

Storage or workspace cost. You probably pay money to rent or lease your home, or maybe a commercial workspace. These are expenses, and the portion of your space you devote to your Etsy business should have a charge associated with it. If your workspace is, for example, 10 percent of your home, the cost is .10 × your monthly rent or mortgage.

Selling fees. Granted, Etsy selling fees are only 20¢ per item, but if you accept payment through PayPal or a merchant account, they, too, take a cut you should factor into your pricing.

Overhead. Marketing your Etsy business takes money—money you need to recoup in order to stay in business. So tally the cost of your website design and hosting, your business phone, your internet access, your photo hosting, and any other miscellaneous expenses in this category you pay to run your business.

As you add up your expenses, you can total them on an annual, monthly, or weekly basis, but eventually you're going to need to divide by the number of pieces you create in that timeframe so you know your basic cost per piece.

Courtney Gifford (etsy.com/shop/lovebuggz) started selling on Etsy in 2010 as a way to show friends and family samples of her handcrafted jewelry. She makes a variety of pieces, but her hand-stamped silver and copper pendants have really caught on.

Courtney Gifford's hand-stamped jewelry is some of her most popular products on Etsy.

(© Courtney Gifford, Lovebugs Jewelry and Lip Balm)

Recognizing that she had a lot of competition on Etsy, Gifford elected to price her products at double the product cost plus a small profit margin. She now has a following, with 50 percent of her customers being repeat buyers. What has worked for Gifford has been "finding a niche—what you like to do that is popular among buyers."

What's Your Time Worth?

When doing something you love, like knitting or drawing or photography, it may be hard to consider charging money for the fruits of your labor. After all, you're enjoying yourself, so should you really expect someone else to pay you for your time investment? In a word, *yes!*

You could be spending that time doing a million other things—cleaning your home, volunteering, reading, working out—but because you chose to invest it in creating products for sale, you need to include the time you spent working as a separate cost.

CRAFTY TOOLS

Keeping track of how much time you spent creating products can be tricky, especially if you switch back and forth between projects. To help you track how much time you're truly spending on your Etsy handiwork, use a timer. Perhaps your smartphone has one you can set. Or you could try a software program such as TraxTime, which you can use to track the time you spend on different aspects of product creation, assembly, and marketing.

Deciding how much to charge for your time can be challenging. Do you charge what you earn on an hourly basis at your day job? That may be too high. Or do you charge minimum wage, which may be too low? There's no right answer, and choosing your hourly rate comes down to deciding what feels right to you.

You can do some research and ask other Etsy sellers how they value their time. You can also investigate what professional artisans in your field, such as seamstresses or woodworkers, typically earn per hour.

At the start, you may simply want to choose a rate that's high enough to compensate you for your time while still allowing you to keep your prices low enough to attract buyers. This rate will be different depending on your product category and price point, and might range from $8 to 25 at the start.

Chris Hwang is a speech therapist by day, plush artist by night, selling her hand-crafted creations in her Etsy store, etsy.com/shop/ChrisCreatures. A seamstress since childhood, Hwang came across a book on plush toys in 2007 and was inspired to make some herself. She turned to Etsy as a way to share what she'd made.

During the 2008 election year, Hwang's Tofu for Obama piece quickly gained popularity, and she sold hundreds at $12 to $15 each. Even more important, she got *noticed*. Now she is regularly invited to art gallery shows, has had her pieces featured in the plush magazine *Stuffed*, and has been commissioned to create custom pieces as well. Etsy helped launch Hwang's career in plush, moving her into the ranks of established and well-respected plush artists.

Pricing Strategies 101

Choosing the most effective price for your products—meaning the price at which you'll attract the maximum number of possible buyers while still being profitable—all comes down to economics. Supply and demand.

Cost Plus Profit

One of the simplest pricing models involves calculating your costs and then tacking on a profit percentage. Called *cost plus* in some circles, it's a straight numbers game. For example, if you sold terrariums that cost $30 to make and wanted to earn at least a 50 percent profit margin, you'd charge $45 per terrarium.

Many government contracts are issued using a cost plus model, which ensures suppliers don't earn an exorbitant amount of money.

Market-Based Pricing

Cost plus is a good guide, but it doesn't take into account market rates for products. Terrariums, for example, may sell for $60, on average, on Etsy. So if you're using a cost plus calculation, you're effectively charging too little. Customers expected to pay—and would have been willing to pay—around $60, and yet, using your pricing model, you only charged $45. You lost out on an additional $15.

Market-based pricing, in contrast, is based solely on what people are currently paying for similar items. To determine your market price, you need to research your competitors, note their prices, and either match their prices or find a way to differentiate yourself so you can charge a little less or a little more.

Although cost plays no part in a market-based pricing model, as an entrepreneur, you need to know what your costs are. Understanding how much it costs to produce terrariums prevents you from pricing them at a loss simply because the market is down right now. So if you know it costs $30 to make a terrarium and your market research indicates buyers are used to paying $28, you'll immediately recognize that you can't afford to charge market rates. You need to charge more than $30 to make a profit.

Market-based pricing is a useful model as long as you confirm first that all your costs have been covered. As long as you know the market rate is above your *break-even point*, it's a good choice.

DEFINITION

The **break-even point** is the price at which all your costs have been recouped, but you're not yet profitable. If your total cost to make a flower wreath is $18, that's your break-even point. At $17.99, you're losing money, and at $18.01, you're profitable. You always want to price your products above your break-even point so you can generate a profit.

Market rates also change as trends emerge and decline and as seasons change. The price of gold has been high for the last few years, for example, making it more costly to design gold jewelry. As a result, silver's popularity has risen tremendously. Similarly, demand for—and the price of—Christmas ornaments starts to climb in November, peaks in December, and falls in January. Keep these factors in mind as you decide what to charge today, and understand you might want to adjust your prices in the future.

Perceived Value Pricing

Perceived value pricing offers the greatest profit potential, but the conditions for perceived value pricing typically only exist for a short period of time.

DEFINITION

A product's **perceived value** is what a customer is willing to pay, regardless of what the product costs to produce. This strategy works best with items in high demand or with art, where the unique qualities of handcrafted products make comparisons and substitutions virtually impossible.

Etsy sellers can price their products higher—much higher—when demand for such items is stratospheric. That is, when people can't get enough of whatever it is you're selling and they're willing to pay an arm and a leg to get it.

Remember ZhuZhu Pets from a few years ago? Every child wanted one for the holidays, and stores couldn't stock them fast enough. Although the retail price was around $10, retailers and individuals who could get their hands on them could almost name their price. Parents didn't want to disappoint their child at Christmas, so they were willing to pay multiples of that price to own one. That's perceived value in action.

Given the unique nature of handcrafted items on Etsy, it's less likely that you'll come across an opportunity to price your products based on the perceived value to the customer. It's more common among brand names.

No matter what pricing strategy you go with, the most important thing is to know your costs and to confirm that you can sell your crafts at a profit. After all, your Etsy store is a business.

Building in Profit

Even if you think you've nailed what your products are truly worth on the open market, or even priced them on the high side, unless you've taken the time to tally all your costs, you could still lose money. Charging $65 for a pair of silver earrings may excite you, but if it costs you $75 to make them, you'll run out of money soon. Likewise, putting a $100 price tag on a mural that took you a month to create won't get you much closer to financial independence.

However, knowing what it costs to produce your pieces and sell them on Etsy is only the first step in your pricing calculations.

Keeping Your Costs Down

Reducing your costs is one way to increase your profit margin, assuming you can keep your prices constant. If, for example, you sell greeting cards for $6 and you can cut your costs from $3 to $2, you've just earned $1 more without any extra work.

Friends Hannah May Halleck and Deb Hepner began recycling shirts into knit skirts a few years ago and found a ravenous market. They buy colorful T-shirts at thrift stores and garage sales for anywhere from 25¢ to $4 and transform them into beautiful women's apparel. To expand beyond their local area, the duo set up an Etsy shop (etsy.com/shop/PrettyStinkinGreen), which became an instant hit.

The duo has recently landed some wholesale accounts in Michigan and Illinois, too. To keep up with demand, and to ensure they're making a profit, the Pretty Stinkin' Green team has raised their prices a few times. At the start, their skirts sold for $30 and took about an hour to construct. Today, the skirts sell for $55 and up.

Being able to buy raw materials for skirts like this for under $4 and sell them for multiples of that price means money in the bank.
(© Hannah Halleck, Pretty Stinkin' Green)

To reduce your costs, go back through your lists of expenses and look for ways you can cut back to be able to lower your prices. For example, can you …

- Find a lower-cost supplier? If you're paying retail, for example, can you set up a wholesale account?

- Switch to lower-cost materials, such as from linen to cotton, gold to copper, or new to old canvases?

- Buy raw materials in larger quantities to reduce your per-unit cost?

- Hire low-cost workers to complete one aspect of your production cost to reduce the amount of time you have to personally invest? Or conversely, can you take back work you had been farming out to reduce your labor cost?

- Move your business into lower-cost space?

- Scale back on your fancy packaging, or create a different way to attractively present your products to buyers, for less?

- Identify a lower-cost supplier for shipping materials, such as foam peanuts or boxes?

- Cut back on marketing expenses, such as advertising or sponsorships, which don't always have a direct impact on sales? Or can you leverage more free marketing tools, such as Pinterest or a blog, to promote your work?

Of course, if you don't have much success in reducing your costs, your other option is to raise your prices. And to support your new high-end position in the market, you might want to make some changes there, too. Instead of cutting back, you might want to tweak your packaging or add a little something extra to help buyers justify paying more for your work.

Increasing Your Revenue

Once you have a solid handle on what you're paying for supplies and extra help and packaging, it's time to step back and contemplate how to make more money from each sale. One way is to reduce costs, as I've mentioned, and the other is to increase the amount of money you make on each sale.

CRAFTY TOOLS

Stay on top of your sales even when you're out scouting for supplies or at the post office shipping orders, with EtsyText, a free app that sends you a text message whenever you make a sale. This mobile app is available at etsytext.com and works with U.S. and Canadian mobile carriers. Be aware that you'll be charged for texts you receive, so switching to an unlimited text plan may be a good idea.

To increase your sales revenue, you can raise your prices or sell more crafts—those are your two options, really. Can you raise your prices slightly, without having a major impact on your number of sales? You might want to test a slight increase to see how customers react.

Or can you support a higher price by making some product changes? Can you tweak your packaging or add a little something extra to help buyers justify paying more for your work?

Can you bundle products to increase the size of each sale, meaning selling more to each customer? The fact that the shipping cost won't go up much at all could be a selling point.

Can you market to customers who have bought from you before and invite them to come look at your new inventory? It's much easier to sell to someone who is already a customer than to try to convince someone to make their first purchase. That's why follow-up sales to existing customers are higher profit—it costs you less to make that sale.

> **CRAFTY TOOLS**
>
> For more guidance in calculating your costs and determining your most effective pricing structure, download *The Art of Pricing for Profit* at etsy.com/ blog/en/files/2012/05/TheArtofPricingWorksheet.pdf. You can also watch a companion workshop presentation on the topic at etsy.com/blog/en/2012/ etsy-success-the-art-of-pricing-for-profit-workshop.

The Least You Need to Know

- No matter how much you love to create, you need to price your creations high enough to at least earn back what you've spent on materials, labor, equipment, and overhead.

- Set annual and monthly financial goals, and calculate how many products you need to sell to reach it. Are you overly optimistic?

- If your customer base is reluctant to pay your prices, find ways to reduce your costs so you can bring your prices in line with what the market wants.

- You have several options when it comes to pricing your crafts. Look at your options and price your work accordingly.

- To earn more profit, you need to reduce your costs, raise your prices, or a combination of the two.

Listing Your Items for Sale

In This Chapter

- Creating sales pages to sell your items
- Understanding Etsy's product categories
- Deciding how far away to sell
- Using keywords to attract buyers
- Monitoring your listing effectiveness

If you've done any online selling at all, at retailers such as eBay, Amazon, or Craigslist, you're already familiar with the listing process. And if this is your first foray into online selling, there's nothing to be nervous about.

By asking a series of questions, Etsy helps you describe your product, determine which product category it belongs in, and organize all the details for you.

In this chapter, you learn all about the Etsy listing process and what you can do to make your listings attract more buyers. Posting items for sale is only half the story; using keywords and choosing appropriate categories makes a big difference.

A Look at the Listing Process

Painter Karen Juneau (etsy.com/people/karenjuneau) has two product lines—hand-painted salt and pepper shakers with a trivet, and oil paintings. She created her Etsy account in December 2011 after her house was so full of paintings, it looked like an art gallery. Upon investigating Etsy, she found "it seemed doable—not too much of a time investment, the price was right, and my work could be seen by thousands of people." Today Juneau works through Etsy because she "doesn't have to spend a lot of time trying to sell my art. Etsy allows me to do as much or as little as I want in terms of promoting or selling." And that's a good thing.

Karen Juneau found the Etsy listing process fairly easy to follow. Although keeping her items, such as this painting, in stock, has been challenging.
(© Karen Guarino)

Your first product listing will probably take 20 to 30 minutes to complete, but by your fourth or fifth listing, you'll be able to fly through it in under 10 minutes. And if you're nervous, just remember you can go back and change anything later if you decide you did something wrong, or come up with an even better description or price. Nothing is permanent.

Once you've set up your online storefront, which lets customers see all your pieces in one location, you're ready to start listing each individual product for sale.

To start, click on the name of your shop at the top of the page on the right. Then choose **Add New Item** from the drop-down menu. That brings up a page that looks like the following screen.

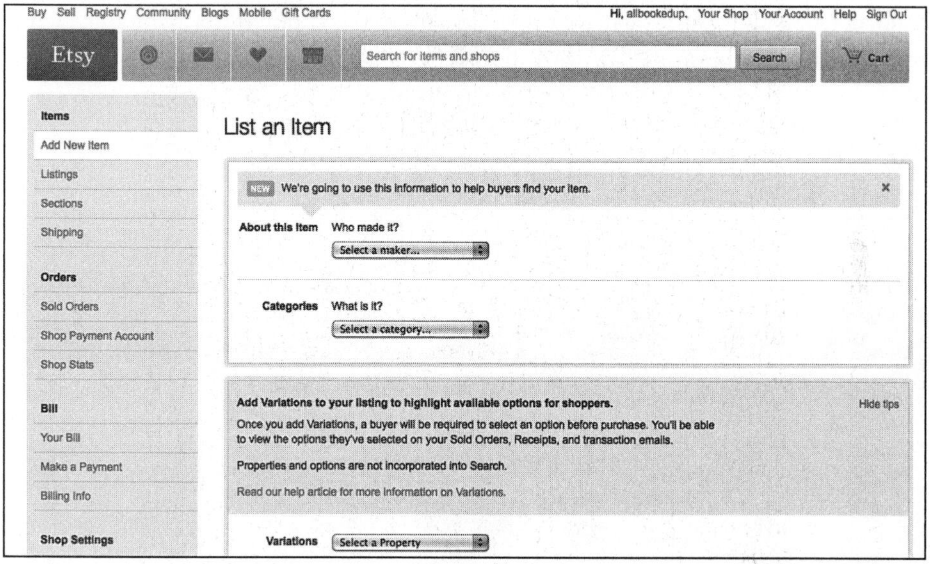

Putting an item up for sale on Etsy is easy and only involves answering a series of questions.

About This Item

Your first question is about who made the item you're listing for sale. Check the appropriate response:

- ❏ I did
- ❏ A member of my shop
- ❏ Another company or person

Unless you have employees or contractors assisting you in creating items, or you're listing already-made vintage items or supplies, your answer should be "I did."

After indicating who made it, another field appears to the right asking What Is It? Your option is "A finished product" or "A supply or tool to make things."

After answering that question, you get a third question: When was it made? Your options include nearly every timeframe imaginable, from "Not Yet Made," to "Made to Order," to "Recently," with specific decades broken down, to "Vintage," which includes decades before 1993. (Boy, do I feel old.)

Categories

The next question asks what type of item you're selling.

Choose the product category buyers are most likely to think of when they see your products.

When you click the menu bar, you are presented with more than 30 different product categories:

Accessories	Housewares
Art	Jewelry
Bags and Purses	Knitting
Bath and Beauty	Music
Books and Zines	Needlecraft
Candles	Paper Goods
Ceramics and Pottery	Patterns
Children	Pets
Clothing	Plants and Edibles
Crochet	Quilts
Dolls and Miniatures	Supplies
Everything Else	Toys
Furniture	Vintage
Geekery	Weddings
Glass	Woodworking
Holidays	

Sometimes, as with mixed media creations, it may be hard to know how to classify your work. So think about how buyers will use it. Will they hang it on their wall? Then I'd call it art. Will they wear it? Then it's clothing. Will they play with it? Then it's a toy. What your piece is made of is less important than what you've transformed it into.

If you can't find a clear category from among the long list, opt for the catch-all "Everything Else."

After indicating your item's category, a field will pop up to the right asking What Type? The choices here vary by category of product. After selecting Art as your category, for example, you'll be asked whether you have a collage, a painting, or a drawing, to name a few responses. If Candles was your category, you'll be asked to indicate if they are Beeswax, Pillar, Soy, or Votive, for example. This field is optional, so if you'd rather not be more specific, just ignore the field and move on.

Photos

Your next step in the listing process is to add up to five photos of the item you have for sale.

I go into great detail about taking photos in Chapter 12, so all you really need to know now is that if you haven't already taken photos, you can skip this step and move on to writing the description, in the next step.

Item Title

Now comes the fun part—telling buyers all about your fabulous piece. This starts with the Item Title, which is like the headline of a newspaper article.

For the Item Title, you want to describe your craft using words your buyer might use to search for it. Mention what it is, its size, its color, what it's made of, what it's used for if that's unclear, how it was made, where it came from, and other names people might call it. Brainstorm how you'd describe it to a potential customer.

Be as specific as you can—such as calling it a "Lot of 20 vintage 1-inch green plastic buttons" rather than just "Buttons." Granted, if you did just call it "Buttons," your listing would probably still come up if buyers searched for that term, but it won't come up first. The closer your title matches what buyers type in the search box, the higher in the list your item rises.

The next step is adding your Item Title, Description, and Shop section.

In addition to describing your craft using common search words, also add alternate spellings or synonyms people might use to increase the odds of your listing being shown to buyers. For example, in addition to "ceramic mug," you also might include "cup" in the title for people who are generally searching for something to hold a drink. If you're listing a "knit top," you might also describe it as a "sweater," "turtle-neck," or "shirt" in the title.

Description

After zeroing in on the most important aspects of your product in your title, it's time to add some detail. Your first paragraph should tell the buyer what it is you have and why they should want to own it.

CRAFTY TOOLS

Etsy's brief article on writing enticing item descriptions is a good primer for creating yours. It's worth a quick read: etsy.com/blog/en/2012/ how-to-write-enticing-item-descriptions.

Your first sentence should be a restatement of your title, maybe with some new information. This is the most important sentence of your description because if a buyer doesn't see what they need information-wise, they may click away to view the next item in their search results. You have a lot of competition on Etsy, so do your best to hook your buyer in that first sentence.

Then detail the item's benefits:

- What will it do for the buyer? Keep their toes warm? Draw attention to their face? Organize their papers? Do a better job of cleaning the windows?

- Will it save them time? Save money? Increase their appeal?

- How will it make them feel to own it?

- If it's a gift, how much will the recipient appreciate it and the gift-giver?

Ask yourself what buyers most want to hear. Put yourself in your buyer's shoes as you write. Do they want to know the necklace is made of 24 karat gold and your 16-year-old daughter will cherish it forever? Would they like to know the wrist warmers you've knit are made of the softest, warmest cashmere on the market? Or are they likely to appreciate that everything featured in your massive mural is repurposed and environmentally friendly? What makes your items unique and distinctive—and better—than other similar Etsy items? That's what buyers want to hear.

Next, use bullet points to tell the buyer more about the item's features:

- Size, which is best expressed as measurements in inches, feet, or yards, rather than vague words like *huge* or *petite*

- Materials used, such as paper, canvas, sterling silver, copper, cotton, etc.

- Technique, especially if you've used a higher-end or more difficult approach to making your pieces, such as serging the seams of your handmade children's clothing or a combination of dry and wet brush painting methods in your art

- Brand name, if you've incorporated a branded product in the creation of your work, such as Swarovski crystals or glass Ball jars

Finally, tell a story about your item. Buyers love stories! Where did you get the inspiration to create it? Do you have personal experience using or owning a similar product? Does it bring back fond memories for you? Did you see one in use somewhere really cool or trendy? Paint a picture of how you created it, or how you see the buyer using it to draw them in and make them want it.

Shop Section

After describing your product in great detail, consider adding it to a section of your shop. Shop sections are really just a way to organize different types of products within your shop. The **Shop section** field gives you 24 characters to describe an individual section.

Morgan Roberts's shop (etsy.com/shop/kingsoleil) has many different types of items, from crochet rugs to embroidery hoop art, and customers for one type of product may not be a prospect for another. Roberts says, "You can use your shop sections to separate a theme. In jewelry, for example, you could have 'Blue,' 'Diamonds,' or 'Metal.' They can be used for fashion shops to denote a season or year, such as Spring 2013 or Winter 2014. You can also add a 'Sale' section or a 'Ready to Ship,' instead of 'Made to Order,'" she says.

Recipient

Because buyers often turn to Etsy for ideas for gift ideas, you can now help direct them to your shop by identifying who your creations are often purchased for.

The complete list of potential recipients includes the following:

Babies	Girls
Baby Boys	Men
Baby Girls	Pets
Birds	Teen Boys
Boys	Teen Girls
Cats	Teens
Children	Unisex Adults
Dogs	Women

This is an optional step, but it's useful if you sell niche products. For example, if you sell pet apparel, you can choose dogs and cats as potential recipients. Or if you make adhesive wall décor for teens, you can identify them as your target market.

We're going to use these new attributes soon to help buyers find your item.
If you currently use tags for recipient, occasion, or style you should continue to add those tags.

Recipient   Who is it for?   optional

Select a recipient...   What if my item is for everyone?

Select a recipient...
Babies
Baby Boys
Occasion   Baby Girls
Birds
Boys   Why only one occasion?
Cats
Children
Dogs
Style   Girls
Men
Pets
Teen Boys
Teen Girls
What will shopp Teens   **r item?**
Tags help shopp Unisex Adults   h on Etsy. Add 13 tags to reach as many Etsy shoppers as possible.
Women

Tags   Add

Add 13 tags. Get ideas.

Materials   Add

Add up to 13 materials used in your item.

Price $ USD

If your products are perfect for gift-giving, the next two fields were made just for you.

Occasion

Similarly, if your items are perfect—and maybe even designed for—a particular occasion, select one in the drop-down menu. You can only choose one, not several.

For example, if you create anniversary poems or mementos, you can help customers find you by clicking on **Anniversary** as an occasion for which your products are purchased. The complete list consists of these:

Anniversary	Hanukkah
Baptism	Housewarming
Bar or Bat Mitzvah	July 4th
Birthday	Kwanza
Canada Day	Mother's Day
Chinese New Year	New Baby
Christmas	New Year's
Cinco de Mayo	Prom
Confirmation	Quinceanera
Day of the Dead	Retirement
Easter	St. Patrick's Day
Eid	Sweet 16
Engagement	Sympathy
Father's Day	Thanksgiving
Get Well	Valentine's
Graduation	Wedding
Halloween	

This field is simply there to help buyers more quickly zero in on products that are appropriate for their particular occasion. If your items work for a wide variety of buyers and events, leave them blank.

WATCH OUT!

Unless your products are typically purchased for a particular recipient or occasion, do not designate one. This is an optional step that will make it more difficult for buyers to find your items for other occasions. But if you specialize in new baby announcements, of course, select that as an occasion.

Style

Another optional field is **Style**. You don't have to use this section, but if your pieces clearly fall into one particular style, tagging them as such will help draw buyers searching for, say, Asian art or cottage chic home décor items.

The final three fields help match your products to buyers looking for something similar.

Fifty-two different styles are listed, and you can choose up to two. You can also add a new style if you don't find your particular blend of fabulous listed.

Tags

You'll hear more about *tagging* and search engine optimization (SEO), which helps attract buyers to your products, in Chapter 11. But when creating your product listing, you really just need to add up to 13 keywords or phrases you think customers will use to search for what you're selling.

Use words that describe what your item is made of, its color and shape, what it's used for, who it's used by, and any other phrase a buyer would use to try to find it. If you have a particular image, such as flowers or kittens, for example, add those, too. All these kinds of descriptive words and phrases are tags.

> **DEFINITION**
>
> **Tagging** is way for online sellers to attach keyword descriptions to products to help connect them with interested buyers. Tagging a cross necklace with terms like *gold, confirmation,* and *baptism,* for example, make it more likely the necklace will come up in a search for those same terms.

Materials

The next field is where you can list up to 13 different materials you used in the creation of your piece. It's very possible you'll only have one or two, which is fine, but add them to the material list to increase the odds your products will come up in a buyer search.

This isn't a pop-up menu with only a limited selection of options to choose from. Instead, you enter whatever materials apply. So whether you work in jade, watercolor, granite, or balsam wood, add those in the **Materials** field.

Price

The **Price** field is self-explanatory: a place to type in your asking price, in U.S. dollars and cents.

Etsy is a fixed-price site, so be aware that this is not an auction where buyers will duke it out to see who is willing to pay the most to own your work. What you type in as your price is what buyers will understand they have to pay to own the piece.

Quantity

The nice thing about Etsy is that if you've worked efficiently and created several of one item, you don't have to create several individual listings if they're all the same. Instead, you simply type in the number of like pieces you have for sale in the **Quantity** field.

Most sellers will probably always type "1," but more power to you if you can crank out half a dozen handcrafted pieces or more at a time!

Shipping

You'll decide later which countries you're willing to ship to, but for now, you need to indicate which country you are shipping from—that is, where you are now. Enter your country of origin: United States, Canada, Australia, France, Germany, the United Kingdom, etc.

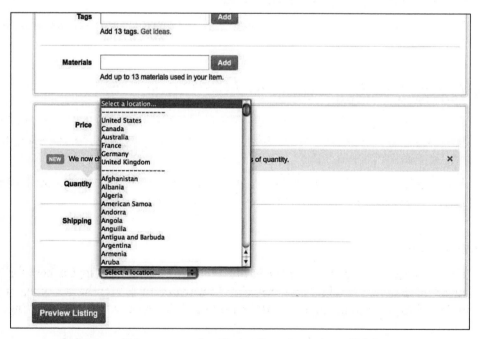

Indicating which country you're shipping from determines which buyers see your listings.

After you've clicked on the appropriate country, you'll be asked to indicate what you'll charge to send the item to someone within your country, as well as what you'll charge to ship it internationally.

I talk about calculating shipping costs in Chapter 8, but the basic approach is to package your item and weigh it. If you don't own a scale, nearly all U.S. Postal Service offices have them and make them available 24/7 in their lobbies, free of charge. When you know your total package weight, you can calculate what you need to charge for shipping to cover your costs by using the online calculator at usps.gov.

Finally, click the blue **Preview Listing** button to see a current draft of your item listing.

If everything looks correct, click the blue **Publish** button at the top of the page. If you see you left something out or want to change something, click the **Edit** button. And if you were only able to input some of the information and you want to come back to it—maybe you decided you need to take a better photo, for example—click **Save as Draft** so you won't lose your work.

Within a few short minutes, your product will be visible and available for anyone on Etsy to buy.

Linking to Etsy Shopping Tools

To sell more on Etsy, you need to be where the buyers are. To do that, you need to be sure your goods are labeled, or tagged, appropriately so customers can find them quickly and easily.

Etsy has a number of shopping tools buyers can use to help sift through the millions of Etsy products and find exactly what they're after more easily.

Categories

The categories you specified in the item listing process are what appear here for buyers in list form. So if a shopper is after knitting patterns and that's a category you indicated for your item, a match will be made and the buyer will see your listing.

Colors

Buyers hunting for tchotchkes to match their vibrant green wall color, or a bracelet to complement their pricey pink cocktail dress, may turn to the Etsy Colors tool to find products matching a particular shade or hue.

The Colors page is really a series of dots of different colors on the color wheel. Click one, and you'll see a seemingly random set of items that are tagged with that color. Yet another reason to be clear about the colors in your items.

Treasury

Treasuries are seller-curated lists of 16 items that run on Etsy's home page, attracting page views like crazy. The treasuries generally revolve around a theme, such as a collection of items made of sea coral, or items that are all bright orange, or all pillows. It's up to the Etsy user to decide how to select and organize their Treasury, which could also simply consist of their favorite items that week.

Treasuries are one of the best ways to help promote and support other Etsy sellers. You can't include your own items in a treasury you create, but by including other sellers' items, you increase the odds that they'll later feature one of your items.

Shop Local

Etsy's Shop Local feature helps buyers find products for sale in their own backyard. For buyers trying to reduce their carbon footprint, reducing the distance a purchase has to travel is big. And folks purchasing larger items, such as furniture, can significantly shrink their shipping expenses by asking to pick up the item instead of pay to have it shipped.

To be sure your town is visible to buyers, enter it in your user profile.

Shop Search

Shop Local presents a series of photos of items for sale locally, and Shop Search shows buyers a list of local shops. They can then click through to peruse the inventory.

Again, be sure your location is public and visible to buyers to take advantage of these useful tools.

People Search

When buyers hear of a seller by name, rather than shop name, they can use People Search to find that individual. Indicating whether the person is a Seller, Non-Seller, or Everyone—meaning, search for either—by typing in a name, all the shops owned by people with that name will be shown.

To be sure buyers can make use of this feature, don't use a variation of your name when you set up your shop, or you won't show up in any searches here.

Prototypes

Prototypes aren't so much tools as they are experiments. Etsy users who think they've built a better way to access or use Etsy can upload their programs here for buyers and sellers alike to test out. Some are new seller tools, while others are new-and-improved shopper tools. This section is more of a testing ground, which may or may not help buyers and sellers connect, and which may or may not exist for very long.

This might sound like a time-consuming task, and although it really isn't once you get going, Etsy seller Elizabeth C. (etsy.com/shop/lizbethsgarden) points out that you can save drafts of listings and publish them later, as long as you've completed each section. You can't save incomplete listings. After you enter all the information you have, click **Preview** at the bottom of the page, and opt to **Save As Draft**. Then you can go back and edit whenever you like before making it live, or making the information public.

Elizabeth C. often creates several listings at a time for her luxury tassels and then releases them over the next several days to increase the number of times she has a new item at the top of the page.

(© 2010 Elizabeth Cogliati)

Defining Your Geographic Area

Most U.S. Etsy sellers have no issues with selling to buyers in all 50 states. Some, however, limit their territory to the contiguous 48 states, simply because shipping fees to Alaska and Hawaii can get pricey.

Others ship to the United States, Canada, and Mexico, our trading partners. Shipping out of the country requires a few extra papers, and a higher shipping fee, but it's not difficult and it certainly broadens your potential market.

When you type in your zip code or city name in your user profile, that information will be used to connect you with people in your geographic area.

Analytics and What They Tell You

Etsy does a very good job of tracking who is checking out your shop. When you click **Shop Stats** under **Your Shop** in the top menu bar, Etsy shares up-to-the-minute details regarding the following:

- The number of visitors to your shop

- The number of buyers who visited specific product listings

- The number of visitors who marked your shop as a favorite (meaning they're much more likely to come back)

- The number of visitors who marked a particular item as a favorite (and who may be considering buying it)

- The number of orders

- The total revenue from those orders

Looking at the graph below those numbers, you can also see where your traffic is coming from. A box lists how your buyers came to you, such as from Google or Etsy, and where they came from within Etsy, such as through a treasury or an item listing. The graph is charted by day, so you can watch for traffic patterns during week.

You can also see keywords buyers used to get to your shop, which can help you spot trending terms you should use more often.

Sellers on Etsy frequently comment on the helpful, collegial atmosphere on Etsy. Rather than being competitive, fellow sellers are eager to help new sellers succeed. The same is true of Etsy corporate. Resources are constantly being added to help you be more successful from the start.

The Least You Need to Know

- Listing an item on Etsy isn't difficult. Just answer a few questions, upload some photos, and you'll be in business.
- The optional fields in the listing process can direct you to hot buyers, but they can also limit who else sees your items.
- Etsy's shopping tools help buyers more quickly find items they're looking for and are an opportunity for sellers to connect with them.

- Etsy Shop Stats provide ongoing and useful details about the traffic you're getting on Etsy and what people are looking at and buying.
- Monitor your stats regularly to spot new keywords you should be using in all your listings, as well as websites sending traffic your way.

Compelling Copywriting

In This Chapter

- Writing what your buyers want to read
- Sealing the deal with persuasion
- Using proven copywriting terms
- Creating attention-getting product titles and descriptions

People come to your Etsy shop in search of beautiful products, but the words you use to describe your work pack a powerful punch. Using phrases designed to entice and persuade, you can push your buyers from "just looking" to "sold" in a few short minutes.

The key is knowing what words to use, and in what order, because if you come on too strong in your sales pitch, you'll push buyers away. Come on too weak, and they'll keep looking for something else that truly inspires them. But when you get it just right, you'll sell more items, faster.

In this chapter, you learn all about the importance of matching your product descriptions to the words your buyers use when searching for items on Etsy. Telling a story, picking powerful keywords, and attracting attention are all covered in the next few pages.

Writing Effective Sales Copy

When writing copy to try to convince buyers to make a purchase, you need to give them what they're looking for right up front, followed by additional information to help them recognize the value you're offering.

Advertising agencies have used the AIDA model forever, and it works on Etsy, too. *AIDA* stands for *attention interest detail action*. It's really four steps to guiding your potential buyer to make a purchase:

1. You start by getting your buyer's *attention* with a headline that stands out.

2. Next, you offer information about your product that's intriguing, captures your buyer's *interest*, and helps them picture themselves as the owner of your craft.

3. Once they're imagining themselves in possession of your piece, you fill them in on the *details*—the specific features and benefits that confirm this is what they want.

4. Then you ask for the order by providing a call to *action*, such as recommending they order it now before someone else gets it.

Put Yourself in Your Buyer's Shoes

In order to write exactly what your buyers want to read, put yourself in their place. Imagine what they're thinking as they're looking at your items. Are they hunting for a birthday present? Redecorating a new home? Trying to find the perfect outfit for their child's first birthday party? Why are they here? What do they need?

Then picture your buyer. Statistics show most buyers on Etsy are women, but what else do you know or can you guess about your average buyer?

• How old are they?

• Do they have children?

• Do they live in a big city, the suburbs, or the countryside?

• About how much money do they make?

• What reasons have past customers given about why they bought your work?

• Why do they come to Etsy to shop?

Certainly there are many more questions you could ask to get a picture of your typical buyer, but these will get you started. Understanding why your customers buy from Etsy, and from you, helps you create product descriptions your buyers can't look away from.

To learn more about your customers, consider creating a quick survey at SurveyMonkey (surveymonkey.com). The service is free if you keep it short, and you could send it with a follow-up note to each customer after a purchase to learn more about them and why they bought from you.

The best way to learn more about your customers is to ask them. SurveyMonkey is a free tool to help you.

Now picture yourself as a buyer shopping at your site. What grabs your eye? What frustrates you? What stands out? What doesn't? How excited do you get when reading the product descriptions? Are they visual, or just the facts? What information do you wish was there? That's the information you need to be sure is front and center for your buyers.

If everything looks good to you, ask a couple friends for feedback. You want to be sure customers have all the details they need to make a purchase decision.

The Techniques of Persuasion

You can draw in buyers and grab their attention in a number of ways. Some of the most popular techniques to use as a lead-in to promotional copy include the following:

Ask a question. "Confused about the different grades of diamonds?" is one example. Your goal is to hit on a question your buyer has been asking themselves in the hopes of getting them to answer "yes" in their head. Then you proceed to tell them about the different grades of diamonds.

Lead with an attention-grabbing statement. For example, "First time ever—the extinct wooly mammoth's fur made into a sturdy ottoman." Other declarative terms along the same line are *revealed*, *why*, and *discover*.

Use numbers in the headline. Numbers indicate exactitude and precision, suggesting you know what you're talking about. So the title, "12 hand-painted bone china plates," is more believable than and preferred to "Set of bone china plates."

Tell a story. Stories are a way to grab attention and pull in someone without much effort. You wouldn't use this in a title, but you could begin your product description with something like, "On my last day in Johannesburg, my tour guide suggested we take a detour …." See, you're already wondering, *Why did he suggest a detour? Where are they going?* That's the power of a story—it draws you in.

WATCH OUT!

Some copywriting gurus advise you to use the word *I* in your copy to help the buyer get to know you better. Don't do it! The most important word to the buyer isn't *I*, it's *you*. Talk to your buyer directly, and let them know you have their best interests at heart. Use *you* as frequently as you can. Leave out *I*.

Must-Use Words Buyers Respond To

Advertising agencies have conducted untold surveys to discover which words are most likely to capture a buyer's attention. The 10 most powerful words in advertising, according to *The Entrepreneur's Guidebook Series*, are as follows:

Discover	*New*
Easy	*Proven*
Guarantee	*Results*
Health	*Safety*
Love	*Save*

I've also heard *free* is an effective word to use.

On Etsy, you'll also want to use words that make your items sound even more irresistible than they are. Generally, that means using descriptive terms. Here are some examples of words you might use to describe your crafts:

> **Colors:** charcoal, fire engine red, ivory, periwinkle, steel
>
> **Materials:** cherry wood, cotton, leather, marble, silk, wool
>
> **Patterns:** brocade, dotted, floral, harlequin, herringbone, plaid
>
> **Sizes:** bulky, gigantic, long, oversized, petite, snug, tiny
>
> **Styles:** art deco, bohemian, classy, earthy, goth, hippie, Asian
>
> **Textures:** buttery, dense, furry, matte, pointy, slick, squishy, velvety

CRAFTY TOOLS

The Etsy blog has a very comprehensive list of descriptive words you can draw from at etsy.com/blog/en/2009/seller-how-to-tag-o-rama-with-descriptive-keywords.

The more you can paint a picture of the item and how buyers will use it or experience it, the easier it will be to make a sale.

So instead of saying, "These dangly gold earrings will look great on you," which is really boring, jazz it up. Help buyers imagine how they'll feel wearing those earrings: "Don't be surprised if all eyes turn to admire you when you enter the room wearing these gold dangly earrings. Not only are they themselves eye-catching, but their shiny glow brightens your face and draws attention to your smile." Can you picture it? That's what you want your buyer to do—picture themselves wearing those earrings. When they can do that, cha-ching! You've made a sale.

If you need help crafting creative product descriptions, take a look at ads from sites like Groupon (groupon.com), for inspiration. Groupon's copywriters can make almost any product sound intriguing.

Using Keywords to Connect with Buyers

In addition to providing an accurate description of your work in your listing, you also want to include the keywords and phrases your buyers are typing to search for products on Etsy. If they're looking for *slippers*, the word *shoe* in your description won't do, because it's more general. Just like *tiara* isn't as specific as *Chihuahua tiara*. (Yes, people do buy tiaras for their pups.)

Your challenge is to find out what those keywords and phrases are and to use them in several places in your product listing. When your description matches the keywords buyers search for, they'll be directed to your shop.

Finding the Best Keywords

Keywords are a mystery to a lot of people. Fortunately, I'm here to take the mystery out of them for you. Many sellers use words and phrases they *assume* their buyers are using to find their products. Sure, these are keywords. But they might not be the *best* keywords, the words lots of other people are using, too. Those are the ones you want.

The only way to learn which words and phrases your buyers use most frequently is to turn to a keyword tool. No more guessing or assuming—you can find out exactly which words shoppers are looking for on a regular basis.

The best way to uncover keywords is to use the Google AdWords Keyword Tool: adwords.google.com/o/KeywordTool. Type in the word or phrase you're thinking of using and Google will tell you how many people searched for it last month, as well as several alternatives that may have better results, meaning they are used more than the term you typed in.

This is what the Google AdWords Keyword Tool search for jewelry *looks like.*

Using Keywords Effectively

After you've typed in the words you were thinking of using in your product descriptions and were given other keywords that are searched more frequently, the next step is to begin writing your product descriptions using those keywords.

You need to use your keywords in a few specific places in order for Google to take notice:

- In your product title
- In the first 10 words of your description
- In the first paragraph
- In your shop description

If you use the primary keyword you discovered, such as *maxi-dress* instead of *dress*, or *durable* instead of *hard*, in these positions, Google will recognize that your product and your Etsy shop are a good match for customers searching for these products or qualities. Your Etsy traffic should increase for the keywords you're using, too. That's the power of proper keyword usage. When you try to match item keywords to what buyers are searching for, it's called SEO, or search engine optimization. By doing a better job of describing your crafts, you increase the likelihood that Google will present your products at the top of its search results—where buyers typically click first.

> **WATCH OUT!**
>
> You certainly want to do your best to match the words you use to describe your crafts with the words buyers use to search on Etsy, but be careful not to go overboard repeating those words. That can actually *lower* your Google ranking. Keyword stuffing or keyword jamming is when you repeat the same word over and over—for example, using the phrase "wool wool wool wool wool mittens"— in the hopes Google will see your item as the very best match for buyer searches. Google is smarter than that, and you'll actually be penalized for doing this.

Writing Eye-Catching Item Titles

Item titles are prime real estate for keywords. They're the first field Etsy turns to when determining if your item fits what a buyer is looking for—it's like a matchmaker. Every keyword that appears is another reason for Etsy to point buyers your way. In fact, it's best to use several together with other descriptive phrases, if you can, to ensure buyers find your listing.

So instead of "gold frame," you might use "huge ornate gold gilt Italian wooden frame." Once you have your keywords in there, the additional descriptors help expand your buyer pool from those who are looking for a gold frame to shoppers who want an Italian frame, or an ornate frame, or a huge frame. With the additional keywords, your title captures all those buyer groups, not just the one you thought you were after.

Avoiding Keyword Jamming

A few years ago, in the early days of the internet, savvy webmasters simply repeated the keyword they knew their customers were using over and over again on the site's home page. So when Google went looking to see which websites were a good match for that keyword, the ones that had hundreds of uses of the word came up higher in search results. The copy made no sense, of course, with so many keywords stuffed or hammered into the product listing, but the websites got a lot of traffic. That's where "keyword stuffing" got its name.

Fortunately, it no longer works as before. Google and other search tools, such as Etsy, wised up. Now you need to have content *that makes sense* on the page, not just words repeated ad infinitum.

That doesn't mean you shouldn't use keywords—you should—but you need to use them in such a way that the Etsy titles and descriptions still make sense to the reader.

For example, instead of keyword jamming the words *crystal vase* 20 times in an Etsy title, a better title would be "Vintage Steuben crystal vase glass etched." Combining specific words related to the product buyers are searching for is much more likely to net you a match than repeating the same phrase over and over.

Matching Occasions

In addition to providing product-specific information in your listing title, also consider using occasion or event-specific words to attract buyers.

For example, if your hats are perfect for weddings, consider adding the keyword *wedding* to your title or your product description. If your handmade fishing lures are generally purchased for men, you might want to add the words *Father's Day gift* to your title and also tag it with those words. That way, anyone who's searching by event, rather than particular product (probably because they have no idea what to buy), will come across your items. (You learn more about adding keywords to photos, called *tagging*, in Chapter 12.)

Abby Leigh (etsy.com/shop/leighandmichael) has a burgeoning Etsy business of handmade children's clothing. She draws subjects like crabs, boats, and dinosaurs; deconstructs the images; and then puts them back together by layering them in appliqué. The effect is very eye-catching. To ensure her outfits come up in searches, she uses keywords that describe the clothing, including the cute images. For example, if a shirt has a flag on it, she uses the word *flag* as well as *Old Glory*, and other words associated with the flag, like *American*, *patriotic*, and *red*, *white*, *and blue*. The more terms you use, the better your search results.

Keywords for this Leigh and Michael Designs shirt could include
toddler, bow tie, *and* formalwear.
(© Abby Leigh)

Penning Perfect Product Descriptions

Now that you've caught the attention of buyers with your oh-so-descriptive product title, it's time to seal the deal with your product description.

Using the inverted pyramid approach to writing—meaning you start talking about the most important aspects of the product first—your product description should read like a news article. Start with the most important facts and features and work your way down to the nice-to-know-but-not-essential stuff. That way, if your buyer only reads the first couple sentences, she can immediately determine if what you have meets her needs. she doesn't have to read 10 more sentences to discover the gloves are wrist-length instead of elbow-length, which is what she was after to begin with.

> **CRAFTY TOOLS**
>
> "Would you like fries with that?" Whenever possible, try to upsell your customers, encouraging them to purchase something else from you that may coordinate with their initial purchase. At the end of a product description for a necklace, for example, you might add, "This necklace has matching earrings. Check them out here [include the link to the earrings]." All Etsy URLs in a product description are clickable, whereas other non-Etsy URLs are not. This is a way to sell more to each customer.

The First 10 Words

Within the product description, the first 10 words are crucial. Those are the words that will make or break you with search engines, including Etsy's.

Be sure you use the most-searched keyword right up top. Those first few words should make it crystal clear to buyers whether your product is right for them.

Repeat, Repeat, Repeat

Within the first few paragraphs of your product description, you should repeat the keywords your buyers are searching for three to five times. Not only does this confirm for the buyer that your product is perfect for them, but it confirms for Etsy and Google that your product is relevant, that it's a good match.

Compelling copywriting takes practice, but once you understand the formula—combine a keyword with other relevant adjectives and repeat three to five times within a description—your shopper traffic should start to climb, and with it, your sales.

The Least You Need to Know

- It's important to do keyword research to find out exactly what your buyers are searching for.
- Once you discover the words and phrases your buyers are using the most frequently in their hunt for similar products, use them in your product title and listing.
- In addition to keywords, *discover, easy, guarantee, health, love, new, proven, results, safety,* and *save* are extremely effective in grabbing a buyer's attention, so sprinkle them in with your keywords.
- The Google AdWords Keyword Tool is the most important website you'll use in researching powerful keywords and phrases that will help you sell more of your items.
- Write product descriptions that make sense, that speak to your buyer, and confirm yours is the product for them.

Photography That Sells

In This Chapter

- Simple techniques for taking great photos
- Lighting how-tos
- Choosing backgrounds that enhance
- Tagging tricks

More than anything else, your photos have the biggest impact on your Etsy sales. You may have the most stunning jewelry, the most gorgeous clothing, or the most intricate wooden home accessories, but unless your photography highlights and showcases it, your sales will falter.

Fortunately, it doesn't take much to dramatically improve the quality of your product shots. By learning some basic photography skills, you can get just the right shot of your item—the shot that will dazzle buyers.

In this chapter, I share helpful tips for taking higher-quality photos without much effort. Better lighting, simpler backgrounds, and keyword tagging are all part of the puzzle.

Basic Photography Techniques

To capture a great product shot, you need to take into account six things: the camera mode, the lighting, the camera angle, the background, props, and showing your item in use.

Camera mode. Yes, you can buy a fancy, expensive camera that has lot of settings and options, but you really don't need that. All you really need is digital camera so you can upload your photos to your Etsy store fairly simply. To make it even easier, the camera should be in automatic mode. Just point, shoot, and shoot again.

Lighting. I talk about lighting in more detail in a second, but the key message here is to use natural light, not the flash. The flash creates a harsh look and can alter the appearance of color, which you don't want. Buyers want to know that the color they see in the picture is the actual color of the item they're buying.

Camera angle. Shoot photos of your item straight on and then try other angles to see which is most attractive.

Background. You can use almost anything in the background of your product shot as long as it enhances the look and feel of the image. White is the most common, but don't feel you have to use white. Soft, mellow shades of most colors help shine a spotlight on your item.

Props. Using props can help create a mood, add color, or show the scale of your work, and for these reasons, you might want to consider them. Just don't use anything that will overwhelm the star of the show—your product—or overshadow it. Keep it simple so buyers focus on your craft item and not the cute tchotchke in the background. Magazines like *Martha Stewart Living* or *Real Simple* can provide helpful inspiration.

Product function. Is there a way you can show how your product operates? Try to use photos to show buyers how your work functions, such as by opening a little door, hanging earrings from a stand, or putting a framed picture on a wall.

Product scale. When it could be unclear to the buyer exactly how big or small your item is, include a prop in the photo to demonstrate. With small pieces of jewelry, for example, a penny or quarter next to your item can show scale. With larger pieces, a ruler or piece of paper can help.

CRAFTY TOOLS

To make your Etsy shop look more consistent and professional, consider creating a "signature" background for all product photos in your shop. By using a single background in every shot, that image becomes associated with you and your crafts. When choosing a background, think about the mood you want customers to feel in your shop. For children's clothes, think about bright, primary colors. For eco-friendly goods, think about incorporating elements of nature. Whatever background you choose, match it to the types of products you make.

The Product Is the Star

Keeping in mind the six components of a good photograph, your goal should be to make your product the star of your shot.

First and foremost, it needs to attract people. If they see one of your photos from a distance, perhaps in a treasury, they should want to zoom in or click through to see more about your work. The item that's for sale in the photo should be extremely obvious, so shoppers don't click through out of confusion to see what the heck that is in the picture.

Using proper lighting, background, and props, your product should direct attention to the work of art itself. Eyes should be drawn to it.

Your product photo should also help answer buyer questions about it, such as, "What is it made of?" "How big is it?" "Is that red or orange?" To do that, zero in on the item's materials, putting a dime or quarter next to a ring to show size, or having a model wear the clothing you've made.

WATCH OUT!

Etsy sizes your photo to 430 pixels wide and crops square images from the center for use in thumbnails, so after you've uploaded it to the site, check your photo's thumbnail. You may need to tweak it to avoid having something cropped out or to fix any distortion that's occurred. Photo editing software, such as Picasa (picasa.google.com), can help, as can online hosting site Photobucket (photobucket.com).

Angle Alternatives

Many Etsy sellers shoot their product photos straight on, much like you would take a family photo—everyone centered in the image, which is taken at eye level.

Most people take these straight-on photos, which are flat and kind of boring.

Taking photos at different angles, however, can sometimes capture a mood or feature you would never get otherwise. Try these other angle shots:

High angle: Take the shot while standing on a chair or stool so you're above your product, looking down. This is an especially good way to capture all of a large piece, such as furniture or art.

Taking photos from above an item can give an accurate perspective of the piece.

Low angle: Take this shot from below, looking up, especially if you're trying to make your product look imposing or dominant.

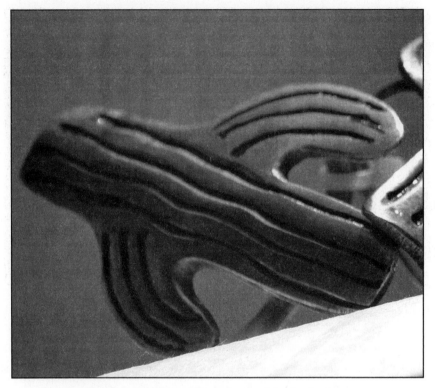

Shooting from below generally makes the object in the photo seem more important or larger than it actually is.

Oblique angle: Whether taken at eye level, from above, or from below, you'll get a more interesting shot from the side.

A sideways portrait of an item is often much more interesting than a mundane eye-level shot.

CRAFTY TOOLS

One of the basic techniques new photographers learn about taking pictures is the "rule of thirds." Using this approach, you mentally divide a square picture into thirds vertically, and then thirds horizontally, so you have a image made up of nine boxes. Then you place the key subject of your shot on one of the imaginary lines or intersecting points for greatest impact. Check out the rule-of-thirds tutorial at digital-photography-school.com/rule-of-thirds.

Close up: When you zoom in on an aspect of your product to the extreme, you've got a close up. This probably wouldn't be appropriate for your main Etsy image, because it won't show the whole item, but it could be a nice additional image to use to show a particular section of your work.

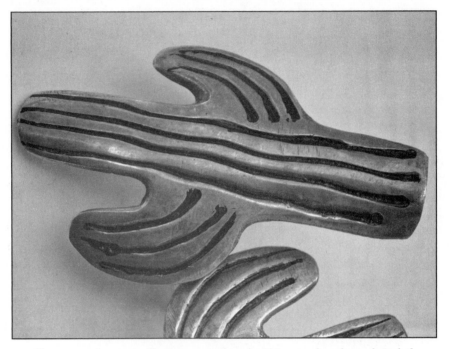

Close-up can be a very effective way to show detail in a product, but only include close-ups alongside full-product shots.

As you're taking photos, keep in mind that they don't have to be aligned perfectly or composed symmetrically. After you've taken the photo, you can use image editing software to crop out sections of the image you don't like, or to really focus the buyer's eye on the product. Picasa is a great tool for easily cropping images. Once you open your image within Picasa, you can rotate it, crop it, lighten it, add contrast, and eliminate red eye—in seconds.

The Importance of Lighting

The one photography element that has the biggest impact on the quality of your images is lighting. You can have the most beautiful piece of art, a dazzling background, an interesting prop, and an expensive camera, but if the lighting is off, none of the other things matter—your photo will look awful.

Proper lighting lets the fine details of your work stand out, rather than being washed out or fading into the background.

Go Natural

The best possible lighting is natural, meaning from the sun rather than lightbulbs or flashbulbs. But even with natural lighting, there's good and bad. Direct, bright sunlight does nothing for your items—it's as bad as a flashbulb—so don't try to take photos at noon on a summer day. The colors of your items will wash out and any imperfections will be spotlighted.

Soft light is the best light for products. Cloudy days or outside shade provide soft light, which smoothes any hard edges on the items you're photographing. The only thing you may not want to photograph on a gray day is the sky, because it will just come out white in your photos.

The best time of day to photograph anything is either at sunrise or sunset. At those times, even if it's sunny out, the light will be softer. Many photographers aim to shoot at between 4 and 5 in the late afternoon.

Another type of lighting, which can make for an even more interesting photo, is backlit, which occurs when the sun shines behind your subject. Unlike soft light, backlighting creates lots of contrast. For that reason, it's best to take photos at the beginning or end of the day so you don't end up with direct overhead sunlight, which is too harsh.

If you can move your items outside to be photographed, that's the best approach, but if not, relocating them on a table next to a window is a very good alternative.

CRAFTY TOOLS

If you want to take your photography a step beyond the kitchen table, the Etsy Entrepreneurs blog shares a great tutorial on how to make your own photo studio. With a few items you can gather from around the house, you can build a very effective studio area. Here's how: etsyentrepreneurs.blogspot.com/2011/02/how-to-make-your-own-photo-studio-on.html.

Setting Up a White Box

I mentioned white boxes in an earlier chapter. With a white box, you can create soft light 24/7. White boxes aren't complex—essentially, they're a smallish box into which you place items you want to photograph. They can make your photography tasks so much easier. When you have a few extra minutes and want to take some photos of your latest creation, you can do it any time of night or day.

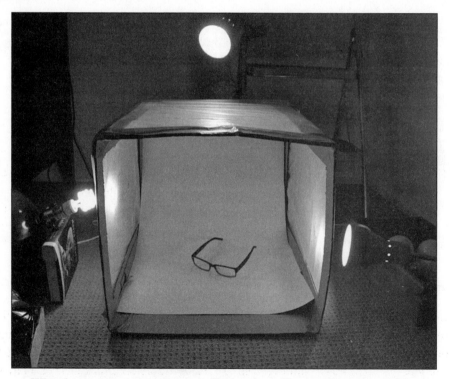

White boxes are an inexpensive and effective way to photograph smaller products.

You can find a number of tutorials for creating a low-cost white box online. (Here are a couple good ones: blog.makezine.com/2006/07/27/diy-light-box and ae.tutsplus. com/tutorials/production/diy-create-your-own-white-box.) In a nutshell, you can use a large plastic storage bin, tipped sideways, some poster board, a couple clamps, and a few lights to make a white box that will make your product images look like they were taken by a pro.

What's in the Background?

What you put behind your craft item can make or break the photograph you take of it. The ideal background is one that helps keep the focus on your creation, rather than detracting from it.

White is a very popular background color for works of art. It won't distort the color of your item, nor will it make your piece fade into the background, like patterns or darker colors can do.

> **WATCH OUT!**
>
> Fancy background images and colors can make for really cool photographs, but using a white background makes it *much* more likely your product will be chosen to be featured in a treasury. Etsians compiling treasuries try to find pieces that look like they go together, and that's a simpler task when the majority of the items are photographed on a white background.

Another option, if white seems too boring, is to use a white background on the first product photo of every item in your shop and then use a different background for the rest of the product photos. That way, the white background will appear first in your set of product images, but serious buyers can click through and see what it looks like against a darker field, with other props, or in place in a room.

Finding Background Sources

Some Etsy sellers create white boxes; others place opaque tracing paper on their window to use as a backdrop; while some look to the floor for inspiration, using hardwood floors or tile as the background surface. Any and all of those options are fine as long as the item you're photographing looks even better against that background in the photo than it does on its own. To know whether that is, in fact, the case, you may need to take some test shots of the item by itself and then against some possible backgrounds.

Other sources of creative backgrounds include the following:

- Scrapbook paper
- Wallpaper books
- Fabric
- Painted poster board or wood
- Carpet squares
- Fine art paintings
- Furniture
- Clothing

Really, anything with a repeated pattern or that's larger than the object being photographed can work. Professional photographers generally order large fabric backdrops from companies like Backdropsource.com or Denny Manufacturing (dennymfg.com).

Also keep in mind the kind of product you're selling and what other colors and textures it may be associated with. Seashell jewelry, for example, could be photographed against a light blue background, to suggest water, or on sand, since that's where seashells are often found. Fur teddy bears could be placed against plaid fabric to suggest the woods or with fabric featuring pine trees. Match your background to your product and the materials they are made of.

Finding Creative Props

Another piece of the photograph puzzle is props. In some cases, adding an extra something to the photograph can help set the mood for the item you're shooting. For example, setting jewelry on a piece of velvet helps create a romantic mood. Placing a rustic planter or two with a sculpture helps buyers understand that the piece is for outdoor use. Or setting a doll next to a stuffed animal shows shoppers it's baby-friendly and meant for children.

Props can help set a mood or define a use for an Etsy item.

Check your home décor for possible props. Also think about what you might have tucked away in your attic or basement. Or check out some of these places for out-of-the-ordinary props:

- Flea markets

- Estate or household sales

- Antique shops

- Garage sales

- Church or nonprofit rummage sales

- Thrift or consignment shops

- Craigslist

- Salvage yards

- Landfills

- Curbs

When looking for props, keep in mind the general style, the color palette, and the general function of your items to find a prop that will work in more than one photograph. If you find a prop that only works with only one of your items, it's probably not worth picking up.

Using Flickr

After you've taken the photos you want to upload to Etsy, you can save them on your computer hard drive, which will quickly fill up if you're serious about being an Etsy seller, or you can upload the photos to a photo- and video-sharing site like Flickr (flickr.com).

Flickr is currently the preferred site for Etsy sellers to store, organize, and share images, probably because you can set up an account for free and upload up to 200 images. Or you can pay $24.95 a year for a Flickr Pro account (or $6.95 for 3 months) and have unlimited uploads as well as stats on your images. Depending on how many items you sell in the coming months, it may quickly become worth $24.95 to have your Etsy images all in one place, and off your computer.

> **CRAFTY TOOLS**
>
> If you're just starting out on Etsy, you might question whether it's really worth the trouble to take that extra step and upload images on a website, rather than managing them right on your desktop. It helps to think longer term. Successful Etsy sellers are constantly listing new items for sale. If you do some simple math, an item a day, for example, will generate at least 150 images a month (5 per listing × 30 days per month). That's nearly a month's worth of images permitted using a free Flickr account. More importantly, that's a lot of computer space dedicated to images.

Uploading Photos

Using Flickr is fairly simple, especially if you've done any kind of work with photos or video. To start, you set up an account at Flickr.com. Then you start uploading images. Once you're at the upload page, you click **Add** and then scroll through your computer files to find images you want shared on Flickr.

*Uploading photos to Flickr is as simple as clicking **Add** and then browsing your files to identify the ones you want copied over.*

When you have some photos stored on the site, you can group them, such as by product type, date, or even color. You also can share them with folks on Flickr, which is another way to draw people to your Etsy shop. And you can tag them for anyone who happens to be searching the Flickr public files for particular images.

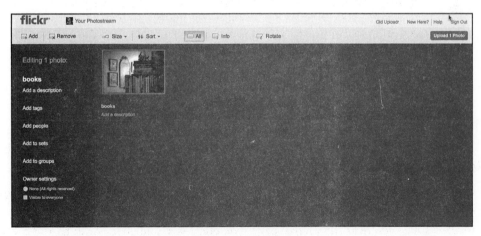

After uploading your images, you can start editing them and organizing them for easy retrieval and sharing later.

Linking Your Photos to Etsy

Once you've created an Etsy listing, take the time to post it to Flickr, too. In addition to being a great place to store images, Flickr is a useful promotional tool, much like Pinterest. You can add a description of the image and keywords to drive traffic to your Etsy shop. Some sellers have had success listing their Etsy shop URL in their About page on Flickr, although you shouldn't try to list it elsewhere on Flickr.

WATCH OUT!

Although Flickr and Etsy have a close working relationship, there are still things you can't do on Flickr to promote your Etsy shop. You can't post a link to your shop in your photo descriptions, mainly, or risk being kicked off Flickr. However, you can still use keywords that will drive people to your item, such as *Etsy, craft,* and *handmade.*

Tagging Tips

Successful photographs on Etsy not only look great but also show up more frequently in searches. By using tags on your photos, you ensure they come up in more search results.

Tags are words buyers frequently use when searching for a particular kind of item, whether it's a *quilt*, or *landscape*, or *trees*. The words you attach to your images help bring them up when buyers search for those words—those are the tags. It's in your best interest to tag all your photos with as many relevant terms as you can. But be as specific as you can; vague terms such as *gift* or *holiday* aren't helpful to buyers trying to home in on, say, a *Bargello belt*. Instead, you'd want to use tags like *Bargello, belt, wool, 36 inch*, and *flame pattern*.

Think of tags as a way to describe your item to someone who hasn't seen it. Be visually descriptive rather than using terms that could apply to hundreds of other items, too, such as *warm* or *pretty*.

What Do Your Buyers See?

The best way to come up with effective tags is to think about how your buyers describe your pieces to others. Is it a *handbag*, a *pocketbook*, or a *purse*? Are the shoes *flats* or *loafers*? Does the canvas feature a *mural* or *painting*? When in doubt, use all the words you think your buyers in different parts of the country or world might use.

But look at your products through their eyes, using their language and terminology. You could even do a search on Etsy and look at how other sellers tag their similar items. Use Thesaurus.com to generate terms that are synonymous, if you're feeling unsure. Ask your friends what they'd call something like what you've made.

Then monitor your shop stats to see what words buyers are using to get to your shop or to your item. If you notice over time that the keyword *peridot* seems to be pulling buyers in, be sure you're using it on each and every piece that features that gem. The same with other listings—use more of the tags that work and less of the ones that don't.

Using Keywords

I talked about keywords and how they work in Chapter 11, so be sure you're using the keyword tools mentioned there to look up the most frequently searched-for keywords. Tagging photos with keywords being used internet-wide, but perhaps not yet on Etsy, can give you a significant leg up.

Be sure you regularly check on which keywords buyers are typing in each month and update your Etsy pages when you spot up-and-coming terms. Also consider naming your photos using keyword combinations, such as *handmade-epoxy turkeys* rather than keeping the image number, something like *DSC0158*, which won't mean anything to buyers.

The combination of a high-quality, clear product photos and descriptive tags will put you head and shoulders above many other Etsy sellers who haven't taken the time to learn the basics like you have.

The Least You Need to Know

- To take an excellent Etsy photo, all you really need is an average digital camera, a grey day, some white poster board, and a prop or two.
- Photograph your crafts outside in the late afternoon and photograph it in natural light against a white background. Or move a table or desk closer to an inside window and take the photo there.
- You can quickly and easily make a white box to hold your artwork while you photograph it.
- Although interesting photo backgrounds can be eye-catching and enhance the look of your product, a plain white background is best.
- Tag your photos with descriptive terms buyers are searching for and keywords you know are popular related to your work.

Keeping Your Finances in Order

Chapter 13

In This Chapter

- Keeping accurate financial records
- Tallying your total expenses
- When to charge sales tax
- Paying your federal taxes on time

You may have the heart of an artist, but you also need to keep accurate financial records. You can't ignore tallying annual sales, totaling your expenses, and paying any income and sales tax owed, even though you may want to. The U.S. government expects you to keep pristine and accurate records of all your expenses and your income so the taxes you pay are correct. That's nearly impossible to do if you don't have a system for regularly logging sales, product costs, and related expenses (like packing materials, shipping expenses, and miles driven to the post office).

Fortunately, although it may be fairly tedious, keeping accurate track of your finances isn't difficult. And if you do it right, you won't overpay on your taxes because you didn't claim all the business deductions you were due. In the end, you'll make more money and keep more of what you earn if you take the time to set up a system for managing your finances.

In this chapter, you learn more about the importance of tracking what you spend to make your crafts and how and when to pay taxes on what you make.

Keeping Track of Your Sales

The most fun part of tracking your finances is watching the top line—the money coming in when you make a sale—grow. Sales are a sign of success, so you want to see a lot of them. That money also creates opportunities for you to buy more raw materials and make more crafts.

Your sales figures are also a barometer of how well your products are synced with Etsy buyer interests. If your items are selling briskly and you can hardly keep up with demand, you know you've got something special and trendy. Do all you can to keep your inventory restocked.

But if you notice your sales have slowed, that's a sign you need to make some changes. Maybe your items are out of season, maybe a competitor is offering a similar product at a bargain-basement price, or maybe your crafts just aren't standing out as much as they need to. You'll need to do some research to figure out what the problem is, but watching your sales will tip you off if something suddenly goes awry.

Using Etsy's Records

Etsy keeps you posted on the value of your recent sales and potential sales from your listings. The **Sold Orders** tab lists all your recent sales, including the sold price and shipping fees.

Find out how much you've made recently from your Etsy sales on your
Sold Orders *tab.*

Establishing Your Own System

You'll also want to set up your own financial management system to combine Etsy's information with other data because Etsy is only one piece of your financial puzzle. The site tells you what you've made, but not what you've spent to earn that money. It doesn't track your product costs or business expenses at all. You have to do that on your own. So use your top line figures from Etsy and then add to them all your expenses so you have a complete picture of what's going on financially in your business.

Some people use Excel spreadsheets, which aren't hard to create and can be modified later if, for example, you find you need to add a new expense category. But adding new information and categorizing can get cumbersome as your business grows.

Others use personal finance software like QuickBooks, which takes some time to set up but automatically sums your income and expenses at tax time. You just have to remember to enter your sales and expenses as they occur, or risk having to play catch-up later, when you might not remember that roll of tape you bought or the special trip you made to buy boxes.

Other software and websites can help, too. One, Outright (outright.com), makes keeping track of your sales, expenses, and taxes due easy. This free online accounting system automatically gathers financial information from your Etsy shop and merges them with PayPal, credit card payments, shipping expenses, and any other manually entered data.

Instead of manually compiling all the pieces of your financial history, try Outright, which pulls them together—for free.

Monitoring Your Costs

Often the key to profitability isn't to sell more items, but reducing your expenses. Some sellers don't seem to worry too much about the cost side of their business, but it can be the key to making money or losing it. Just because you have lots of money coming in doesn't mean you aren't spending even more than you're making. To be sure you're in the black (versus the red), it's important to watch your spending.

Your Etsy Sold Orders tab tells you what's coming in, and your bank account, PayPal account, and credit card statements, together, can tell you what's going out. What's left is your profit.

WATCH OUT!

What you spend on your business isn't really your only expense. Your time is another component to consider. When you invest your time in your Etsy business, you're giving up the opportunity to invest it elsewhere, such as on your full-time job or with friends. It's possible for Etsy to become all-consuming, and that may not be best for your sanity or your bank account.

To stay in business long-term, or even just to make it worth your while to sell on Etsy in the short-term, you need to be sure your profit figure is always positive. There's no such thing as losing a little on each sale and making it up in volume, as accountants often joke. If you're losing money on one sale and work to ramp up sales, you'll only lose bigger. So be sure you're in the black on each and every item sold.

The simplest way to break down your costs by individual item is to use an Excel spreadsheet to tally your expenses per product. Create a page with a column for each product you've created. Then subtract your direct expenses per item. Your direct expenses are those associated with your crafts—raw materials, tools, shipping expenses. The more products you make, the higher your direct expenses.

If you can't separate costs easily for each item, divide the total by the number of items you'll be able to make with it to get an individual product cost. So, for example, if you bought a skein of yarn and expect to be able to make two items from it, the cost of the yarn needed for one product is $1/2$ of the total cost of the skein. Or if you bought a huge bag of beads and will be able to make seven bracelets from it, the cost per bracelet is $1/7$ of the total cost of the bag.

Your direct costs can include, but are not limited to, the following:

- Supplies

- Mailing labels, boxes, printer ink

- Etsy and PayPal fees

- Travel costs to buy supplies or mail products

You also need to assign a portion of your indirect expenses to each product. Your indirect costs can include the following:

- Tools needed to create, such as glue guns, knitting needles, and paint brushes

- A dedicated phone line

- Your internet access

- Costs for accounting, legal, or marketing help

- The cost to attend educational programs, such as an Etsy Craft Party or blogging conference

Tally your total costs for your indirect expenses and divide it by the number of items you created. Subtract that cost from the sale price of each item, and you'll be able to tell if you made a profit. Calculating this monthly is a good way to confirm you're making a profit or be alerted to rising costs before you start losing money.

To accurately monitor how much your Etsy shop is generating, you need to track sales *and* costs.

Collecting Sales Tax

Another figure you'll need to keep track of is the sales tax owed on any of your sold items. Unless you're located in Alaska, Delaware, Montana, New Hampshire, or Oregon, where no sales tax is charged, you'll want to be sure you're following your state's regulations for the collection of sales tax. If you don't, the state can come after you later—even years later—for the sales tax you should have collected but didn't. It's best if you just start collecting and paying it to the state now.

As of July 2012, if you're currently making less than $4 million a year and sell a product to someone else in another state, you don't need to collect sales tax. It's only when you sell something to someone *in your own state* that you need to collect sales tax. Many discussions are taking place right now to change that policy and require all online sellers to collect sales tax from everyone, no matter where they're located, but as of this writing, you only need to collect sales tax from others in your state. To be sure you're collecting sales tax appropriately for your particular state, check the website for your state's Department of Commerce.

To collect sales tax, the first thing you need to do is register for a state sales tax permit. It may also be called a resale certificate or resale number because one of the benefits of getting this permit is that you won't be required to pay sales tax on supplies you buy and use to make new products for sale.

CRAFTY TOOLS

Online and eBay seller Skip McGrath has compiled a helpful list of links to take you to your state's particular sales tax request form at skipmcgrath.com/articles/ salestax.shtml.

Setting Your State's Sales Tax Rate

When you have your sales tax permit, it's time to start adding a tax payment to your Etsy sales to buyers in your state. Fortunately, most states allow you to charge your local tax rate, rather than make you become familiar with the tax rates of every state in the nation. This isn't true in Washington State, however, where you're required to charge the buyer his or her local tax rate.

Here's how to set your local state sales tax rate in Etsy:

1. Go to **Your Shop**, click the **Shipping & Payment** tab, and select the **Sales Tax** tab.

2. Choose your state.

3. Enter your county's tax rate in decimal form—that's 7.25, not 7¼. To find your county's tax rate, check with your state's Department of Revenue.

4. Click **Save**.

Charging sales tax through Etsy is relatively painless when you set it up through the ***Shipping & Payment*** *tab.*

Any buyers in your state will be charged your local tax rate, and any buyers who aren't in your state won't be charged any sales tax.

As you start to collect sales tax, it would be smart to set up a separate bank account specifically for sales tax. As you make a sale, transfer the sales tax amount into that separate account. This ensure the funds will be there when it's time to pay your taxes.

Remitting Your Sales Tax

Check with your state to learn when you should remit what you've collected. Some states expect it monthly and want it electronically. Others collect quarterly and you can mail a check.

To be sure you're giving your state what it wants, when it wants it, do a Google search to figure out when and where to make your payment. Some states even offer discounts for prompt payment, so take advantage of that whenever you can to keep some of that money in your business.

Keeping the Tax Man Happy

In addition to paying your state sales tax, you also need to pay the U.S. government its portion of your earnings, a.k.a. income tax.

Your legal business structure determines when you need to pay your taxes. Sole proprietors, for example, pay at different times than partnerships, LLCs, corporations, and subchapter s corporations.

Most Etsy crafters start out as individual sellers, rather than as businesses, and should report any income they earn as part of their personal income tax filings. But if you've taken the step to formalize your business, how it's structured dictates when you should pay taxes. Some sellers decide to set up a legal business, meaning a limited liability company (LLC), corporation, partnership, or DBA once they're generating tens of thousands in revenue and want to protect their personal assets.

Partnerships, S corporations, C corporations, and LLCs should all be formed with the help of an attorney. Sure, you might be able to figure out how to complete the paperwork yourself, but an attorney can help you decide which structure suits your needs best.

If you operate a DBA, which means you've filed a Doing Business As form and operate as a sole proprietor, you're expected to pay quarterly estimated taxes based on what you've earned. Most Etsy sellers work as sole proprietors. Here is an article on paying taxes as a sole proprietor: biztaxlaw.about.com/od/taxesonbusinesstypes/f/solepropincometax.htm.

 WATCH OUT!

Your federal income tax is different from your withholding tax, which is calculated based on what you pay your employees and yourself. Withholding funds are due monthly, paid electronically, and are calculated based on what you paid out in salary and wages to anyone in your business. Don't get the two taxes confused.

If you operate as a partnership, LLC, corporation, or subchapter S corporation, you may pay at different times based on either your company's income or your partners' proportionate earnings.

The Least You Need to Know

- While your focus may be on selling, keeping track of what you sell and what it costs makes the difference between staying in business and shutting down.

- In addition to monitoring your sales, pay close attention to how much money you're spending to get those sales. If you lose a little money on each sale, you'll lose a lot in total.

- The current law requires you to collect sales tax, and remit it to the state, when selling to someone in your state. If you sell to a buyer in another state, you don't have to collect sales tax.

- All businesses pay income tax to the U.S. government, but how much and when depends on your business's structure. Check with the IRS to determine when and where to send your payment(s).

Marketing Your Etsy Business

It's very possible that your crafts will be noticed by a buyer on Etsy and purchased within a matter of days. The website does get 42 million unique visitors each month, after all. However, the most successful Etsy sellers regularly invest time marketing their Etsy shops to attract buyers and sell more of their work.

Etsy does a great job of bringing buyers to its site, but it's up to you to entice them into your shop. Etsy helps, by providing ways to showcase your work, such as by being included in a treasury on the Etsy home page or by being a featured seller. But you can take plenty of other steps to promote your work.

Social media is a smart starting point because you can reach hundreds or thousands of people with a few clicks of a mouse. Share photos of your work on Facebook, tweet about your newest creation on Twitter, pin your product photos to Pinterest, and blog about your latest inspiration. Each time you share information about yourself and your work, you forge connections with potential customers.

Marketing to attract new customers is one way to build your Etsy business, but keeping in touch with people who have already bought from you is even more important. It's much easier and more cost-effective to sell more to someone who is already a fan.

Pulling in Customers

In This Chapter

- Tips for wowing buyers
- Staying connected with your customers
- Creating profitable promotions
- Building a repeat clientele

It costs between five and eight times more to attract a new customer than it does to sell to someone who has already bought from you. So although there are less-expensive things you can do to attract buyers and persuade them to do business with you, it's so much more important for your Etsy business to think long term.

Knowing up front that your goal is to identify prospective customers and foster a relationship with them that spans years, not days, shapes the kind of marketing strategy you develop for your Etsy shop. As in dating, the approach you take to finding and developing relationships with people you hope will be around for a long time is very different from finding people willing to buy from you, or date you, just once.

In this chapter, I share tips for making first-time customers long-time customers and how that can positively affect your bottom line. Building a solid customer base can help even out your sales and provide a steady income stream.

Giving Your Customers a Little Something Extra

When someone buys from you, they prove they like your work and are willing to pay for it. That's a big step. Because once someone buys from you, if they like what you've sold them, they're likely to buy from you again and to spend even more with you. With each purchase, that customer becomes more and more valuable to your business.

But what can you do to convert someone from a sales prospect to an official customer? Plenty.

If someone comes across your Etsy shop, it's either because they did a search for something, such as placemats, and your shop came up as a potential source of placemats, or because someone else told them about your work and they looked you up by name. Either way, understand that it's very rare for someone to randomly find you out of the blue. It's much more likely that they'll be looking for something specific and just happen across your shop.

Of course, that's great news! That means the majority of your potential buyers are prequalified—they know what they want, and you match some aspect of their shopping search.

On Etsy, you generally won't find buyers milling about. Sure, plenty of people come to explore Etsy, but they frequently have a purpose or a goal in mind. Most Etsy buyers aren't tourists wandering into your shop because they're exploring the area and have no idea what you sell, as with a brick-and-mortar store. Most buyers who explore your Etsy shop are there because you work in a material they like, such as copper; use a creative process they admire, such as appliqué; have a collection of pieces in a color they love, such as celery green (my favorite); or are looking for ideas in a particular product category, like furniture.

Some consumers will stop by your shop and leave because you don't have what they were looking for. That's fine, because at least they got a sense of what you specialize in and are good at. A segment of that group of shoppers will like what they see, even if you don't happen to have what they're after today, and will want a way to see what you list in the future. So they may make you a Favorite shop, or they click on a particular item that interests them and identify it as a Favorite, which lets you know they like you and are looking for a reason to buy from you in the future.

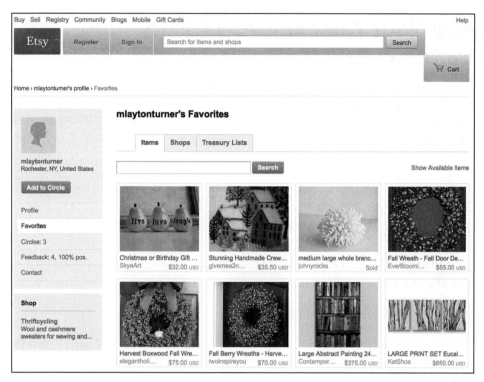

The number of times buyers have added items or your Etsy shop to their list of Favorites is a sign of your growing popularity.

WATCH OUT!

When someone makes your shop or one of your items a Favorite, do not take that to mean they want to hear from you. Do not automatically add them to your mailing list or make contact. Maybe they just like the ceramic planter you made and are considering buying it—and that's all. You shouldn't ask permission to keep in touch with them until after they buy from you.

Another segment of shoppers will like what they see and decide to buy from you on the spot. As part of your packing and shipping process, you may consider adding a note in their package asking if you could add them to your mailing list so you can keep in touch. You can ask them to email you with permission, or sign up on a separate web page, called a squeeze page, that offers additional incentives for joining the mailing list. The purpose of the squeeze page is to encourage visitors to sign up to be on the email list.

Or you can do what more and more information marketers do and include a note that as a bonus for their purchase, they have been automatically added to your VIP mailing list, qualifying them for special offers and promotions. As of today, that approach is legal, but you also need to provide an unsubscribe link in any future communications so those folks who don't want to be on your mailing list can immediately get off it. Be aware that some customers might think it's pushy of you to add them to your mailing list without checking first.

WATCH OUT!

The CAN-SPAM Act of 2003 made it illegal to send email messages to people who did not request contact from you or with whom you have never done business. If you've done business, you're okay, although you always have to give them a way to immediately unsubscribe. Find the full regulations at business.ftc.gov/documents/bus61-can-spam-act-compliance-guide-business.

Offering Free Information

One way to encourage people to sign up for your mailing list is to offer freebies. Shipping and mailing sign-up gifts can get pricey, so consider offering free information instead subscribers can download.

This free information could come in the form of a special report, a checklist, a set of tips related to making a purchase decision, a schedule of events, or even an ebook. For example, if you sell clothing, you could offer a seasonal report on what styles are going to be hot next season. Or a guide to choosing clothing that best fits your body type. Or a checklist for the basic pieces of clothing you should have in your closet.

The more timely and interesting your free information, the greater its perceived value and its ability to persuade customers to sign up to be on your mailing list. Information that's obvious, unwanted, useless, or boring is unlikely to do you much good.

Think carefully before offering a freebie someone else has created, too. Promoting someone else or their brand doesn't really help your business, unless the free information isn't generally available and the author is well known and fairly well respected, such as Martha Stewart or Oprah or Chef Bobby Flay. In that case, being associated with the celebrity might boost your brand authority. Just be sure what you're offering hasn't already been plastered all over the internet. For your freebie to have value, it can't be viewable elsewhere without having to subscribe.

Including Purchase Bonuses

In addition to working to add potential customers to your mailing list, there are other ways you can surprise and delight new customers—or any consumer who buys from you.

Who doesn't like getting an unexpected gift?! Like the *amuse bouche* (a free bite-size hors d'oeuvre provided at the start of a meal) a chef sends over to a customer's table at upscale restaurants, a bonus gift sent with a purchase can make you more memorable and enhance your buyer's purchase experience. Companies have built entire businesses with this concept, which you should seriously consider using in yours.

Most customers will place greater value on a handmade bonus item, but don't feel your freebie has to be handmade. Decide whether it's worth your time to create something else to mail or if you should buy something already made. I included a list of possible freebies provided in Chapter 8, but here are a few more to get you thinking about what might work best for you:

- A small metal clip to go with scarf
- Monogrammed stickers to be applied to stationery
- Push pins to accompany a bulletin board
- A jam spreader to accompany homemade jellies
- A set of coasters to accompany wine glasses
- A small bottle of leather protector to accompany leather products

You can also vary your bonus by season, sending every buyer, no matter what their purchase, the same thank you gift. For example, in the winter, you might send a pair of inexpensive knit mittens or gloves. In the spring, maybe you include an umbrella or a flower-growing kit. In the summer, you could include bug spray or a pretty flower vase. And in the fall, you could tuck in a jack-o-lantern carving kit or use colorful leaves as packing materials.

Although you certainly want to increase your customers' preference for your Etsy shop, be careful not to overspend on bonuses or freebies. Don't spend too much of your profits on items your customers aren't expecting in the first place.

If you're a new Etsy seller, you may want to pay for such freebies yourself, considering them an expense needed to grow your business. Or you could simply increase the price of each item by enough to cover the cost of the freebie so you're not losing money. Either approach is fine, as long as you're not losing money by throwing in the freebie.

> **CRAFTY TOOLS**
>
> Some marketers turn to direct-mail catalogs of lower-priced items for inspiration when looking for bonus items. Oriental Trading (orientialtrading.com) is a favorite because you can buy in bulk for very reasonable rates.

If you decide to send a free bonus item to your customers, be sure they don't overlook it as they unwrap their purchase. Put it on top of your shipment, and mention it in a little thank you note so it doesn't get lost and tossed.

Keeping in Touch with Your Customers

After you've made a few sales and—with their permission—collected some contact information from delighted customers and admiring fans, you'll want to set up a database of customer contact info. You can create a simple Excel spreadsheet, or if you sign up with a shopping cart system like 1ShoppingCart (1shoppingcart.com) or a mailing list manager like MailChimp (mailchimp.com), those sites will automatically create a file of customer emails for you.

Stay in touch with your customers and fans regularly. There's no point in setting up a database, adding names of new customers, and then never referring to it again. The whole idea of creating a customer database is to communicate fairly regularly with people who like your work.

The best tool to keep in touch is an email newsletter. Just like a printed newsletter that arrives in the mail, an enewsletter shares information with customers and invites feedback, but through email, not the U.S. Postal Service.

The primary benefit of an enewsletter is its low cost. You may spend a little money each month to subscribe to an email delivery service, but that's it. Assuming you write your newsletter yourself and take your own photos, the relative cost is minimal.

Some of the most popular enewsletter subscription services, which typically provide newsletter templates and advice for writing and sending issues, include the following:

- 1ShoppingCart (1shoppingcart.com), which does more than newsletters

- Aweber (aweber.com), another service offering more than newsletters

- Constant Contact (constantcontact.com)

- Craftmonkey (craftmonkey.com)

- iContact (icontact.com)

- MailChimp (mailchimp.com)

Definitely take a look at Craftmonkey. This app combines MailChimp with Etsy so you can create your own email newsletter and send it straight from your Etsy shop in no time.

CRAFTY TOOLS

Download a free comprehensive guide to marketing your Etsy shop using MailChimp from mailchimp.com/resources/guides/mailchimp-for-online-sellers. And check out Mashable's nice review of more than 30 mailing list services at mashable.com/2007/08/10/email-newsletters.

When you have your enewsletter service lined up and your database full of names, what do you do next? Think about what you'll write about.

Sharing News

Enewsletters are great for sharing news about you, your latest craft creations, and interesting factoids related to what you sell. Information builds trust and familiarity, which fans the flames of consumerism—the more people know, like, and trust you, the more they'll want to buy from you.

To decide what you'll write about in your newsletter, start by picturing your typical customer. Who are they, what are they like, and what would they want to hear about? Don't create a list of enewsletter topics based on what you want to write or say; start with your customer in mind instead.

CRAFTY TOOLS

If you're a crafter who blogs, be sure you invite blog visitors to sign up for your newsletter there, too. Add a sign-up form to ayour blog's side column, for example, to continue to build your list of fans of your work. Drawing people to your email list from a variety of sources is smart.

Personal information. Because they've bought something from you or signed up for your newsletter, they're obviously interested in you and who you are. So spend a little time in each newsletter sharing personal information about yourself that your customers might find interesting. That last part is key—really think about what you can share that will be interesting and give people a peek into your private life, without oversharing or, conversely, being downright boring.

Do tell them about …

- A trip you recently took, especially if you can tie it back to your products.

- An upcoming vacation you're planning.

- An inspiring event you went to, or a craft fair you participated in with great results.

- A mentor or inspiring person you recently interacted with.

- Happenings in your neighborhood that are entertaining or shed some light on what it's like to live where you live.

- Your family, but be careful not to share too much about your children and their schedules—it's just not safe.

- Your pets and crazy or cute things they've done recently, especially if you've a related fun story about a project you were working on.

You can do this in a short welcome message somewhere in your newsletter, to give your customers a sense of who you are and how you spend your days.

Do not tell them about …

- Bad news you've received, unless you can explain how you turned it into good news.

- Medical procedures you've had.

- Your political or religious views, or any topic that's currently controversial—you want customers to like you, not get mad at you.

- The weather and other subjects readers might react to with, "Who cares?"

Craft-related details. In addition to letting readers get to know you better, use your newsletter to demonstrate your expertise and skill in your craft area. So tell them about …

- How you select your raw materials.

- Where your ideas for different pieces originated.

- How your production/crafting process is different from or better than the typical approach.

- Where and how you received training.

- New techniques you've tried and whether they were successful or not.

- Examples of similar work you admire.

Today, images are even more important than words in newsletters, so try to include photos of your finished pieces or works in progress so your customers understand how much time and energy you put into each item.

Benjamin Coleman created the free online magazine, Origami Bonsai, *as a way to attract people to make origami bonsai structures, but it actually bolstered his status as an origami expert.*

News related to your creations. Sometimes people who buy your crafts are interested in hearing more on related topics. For example, if you sew extra-absorbent dish towels, you might find that your best customer is environmentally conscious and eager to give up paper towels. If so, you could include a short news item or tip in each enewsletter issue about saving money while saving the earth.

Or if you make papier-mâaché Saint Joseph statues for home sellers, you could include other tips related to home selling. If you make hair ribbons for children who show horses, you could include tips related to successful horse showing or pony care. If you make hand-stamped jewelry for new moms, you could include some tips for helpful tools and gadgets for new moms.

Think about who your best customer is and whether he or she has a particular lifestyle or area of interest that might be a source of future articles. Sometimes there will be, and other times your customer base will be so heterogeneous you'll need to keep your tips and information kind of generic.

Your latest pieces. Another key section you'll want to be sure you include in each issue is something about your most recent creations. Your goal is to show your potential and current customers your range of skills and entice them to buy, or to buy again.

You might have a photo and a description of a recent custom piece you made that was a little different from your typical item. Or an image of an item you just listed for sale, with a little description about why you're proud of it. Showcase your favorite latest creation, and tell your readers why it's special.

Encouraging Follow-Up Purchases

By staying in touch with prospective and past customers via an enewsletter, you're helping keep you and your shop at the top of their mind, which is step one in earning a second purchase. By sending a newsletter, even if it's never opened and read, your buyers will at least see your name in the email From: line and be reminded of who you are and what you sell.

Statistics vary on how many contacts it takes before a prospect makes a purchase decision, but it's somewhere between six and nine separate messages or touches. So each time you distribute your newsletter, you're moving your potential buyers closer to familiarity with you and closer to deciding whether to do business with you.

That doesn't mean that after eight newsletters they'll suddenly buy, but at that point, they'll have considered your product and whether it meets their current needs.

Be sure every newsletter issue contains a clear call to action: a suggestion to read a recent blog post you wrote, a coupon code to do some shopping, a poll that's timely or related to your crafting specialty, or a question you'd like customers to answer, perhaps about their preferences as they relate to what you create. Use your newsletter to spawn additional interaction with your potential buyers, which will also help deepen their relationship to you.

Offering Promotions

Your beautiful crafts will often be enough to attract buyers, but if you want to jumpstart sales, consider using some promotional techniques.

In today's coupon-collecting, bargain-hunting environment, some buyers have been trained to wait for an offer they can't refuse. So what can you do to sell to them? Give them an offer they can't refuse.

Enticing with Incentives

One of the easiest ways to do that is to announce a bonus with purchase, much like the freebies we just talked about. It's nice to get a surprise, but it's also possible that knowing they will receive a little something extra will be enough to push a buyer into clicking the Buy button.

Here are some examples of incentives a few Etsy sellers came up with to offer their customers, which were discussed on an Etsy forum.

Creating Coupon Codes

If you'd rather give a percentage off a purchase, you can easily create a coupon code buyers enter at checkout to take a percentage off their purchase price or get free shipping, which can also be a big purchase incentive.

To set up a coupon, go to your shop and click **Coupon Codes**. On the next page, click **Create New Coupon**, which will bring up this box:

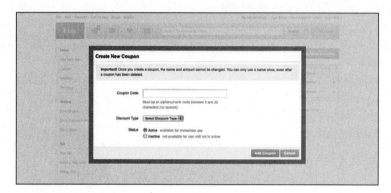

Creating a promotional coupon code takes seconds but can give your Etsy sales a major boost.

Next, enter a 5- to 20-character alphanumeric code buyers can use to enjoy the savings you're offering, such as SAVE20 or GRADUATE. Each code needs to be unique—you can't use codes from previous promotions.

Then select whether you want the code to be for a percentage discount or free shipping. If you're setting up a percentage discount, a new box will pop up in which you can enter the percentage savings you're offering.

Etsy assumes you want to activate this code, so the **Active** button is filled. Then click **Add Coupon**, and your code can be used.

Of course, no one will know about the code unless you tell them, so consider mentioning it in your next newsletter, adding it to your Shop Announcement, or typing it up on a packing slip and giving it to customers in their shipments to entice them to order again soon.

CRAFTY TOOLS

Don't just call your coupon code a coupon code. That diminishes it. Instead, position it as a special deal for your special fans. Let newsletter subscribers know they're receiving this coupon because of their relationship to you. Call it a "VIP discount" or "exclusive offer" to remind your email list that this savings opportunity is a perk for subscribing.

You can decide when to stop the promotion by simply going back to the **Coupon Code** box and clicking **Inactive** to disable the code. It's generally best to advertise savings for a particular time period, such as the month of August, or around a certain event, such as Valentine's Day. Knowing there's a deadline will lead to fewer disappointed customers and may get them to act now, rather than later.

If you're offering free shipping, you may want to put limitations on it, such as only domestic shipping, only the contiguous 48 states, or only United States and Canada. Although international orders can bring you a substantial amount of business, the shipping costs may eclipse the value of the purchase, so be careful as you write up any exceptions to your coupon code.

Why Repeat Customers Are Critical

Enticing buyers to purchase one of your crafts can take time, money, and effort, so once you've identified someone who likes your work, do what you can to keep in touch and give them the opportunity to do business with you again and again.

Doing more business with existing customers is less costly, so invest more resources in convincing satisfied customers to buy from you again than in trying to find new customers interested in what you have. Yes, you need customers new and old, but in the long run, you'll make more money from the old. Just keep that in mind as you start developing your promotional strategy.

The Least You Need to Know

- Focus on establishing long-term relationships with customers so they'll buy more than once.
- Create a database of prospective and current customers by asking them to register at your site or sign up for a free newsletter or report.

- Offering purchase incentives, such as bonuses or extras, can be a useful tool for encouraging sales.

- Sending newsletters makes it easy to keep in touch with your buyers and fans on a regular basis.

- To encourage purchases, set up a coupon code that gives them a percentage off their purchase price or provides free shipping.

Chapter 15

Etsy Marketing

In This Chapter

- Leveraging Etsy's promotional power
- Joining groups and creating treasuries
- Wooing the media
- Applying for awards

You may be surprised to learn that one of the best places to market your work is right on Etsy. Sure, you can invest time and money promoting your skills and your work elsewhere, but before you do that, be sure you're taking advantage of all the free promotional opportunities Etsy has to offer—and there are a bunch.

If you think about it, focusing your initial marketing efforts on Etsy makes a lot of sense. Etsy already attracts millions of buyers each day who are window shopping or ready to spend their hard-earned cash, so why not do all you can to snag their business? Etsy provides its sellers several ways to be seen by buyers, so be sure you're using these resources before you spend money on other marketing tactics.

In this chapter, you read about effective promotional tools and tactics you should be using to bring attention to your Etsy shop, including collaborating with fellow Etsy crafters.

Spreading the Word Around Etsy

Etsy's crafting community is very collaborative, not competitive, which means other sellers are very willing to help promote you. In fact, Etsy seems to have built in that support.

You can join teams to support and promote each other, involve friends and customers in keeping up with what you're working on, go to in-person Etsy events to learn new techniques, subscribe to one or more of several Etsy newsletters, or tune in online for tips and skill-building.

Or not. All these learning and support opportunities are completely voluntary, so if you don't want to take advantage of Etsy's many promotional tools, you certainly don't have to. But they're free and have been shown to be effective, so why not?

Joining Teams

One of the absolute most effective resources Etsy offers its sellers is the opportunity to create and/or join teams of fellow sellers. For more information about teams, click **Community** on the Etsy home page, and click **Teams** in the left column.

You can join one team or several, keeping in mind that some teams set expectations regarding each team member's participation. Teams may ask members to create a new treasury each week (which is time-consuming when done well), commit to promoting a certain number of team members on social media (which can also be time-consuming), and maybe identify themselves or tag their items as members of a particular team.

> **WATCH OUT!**
>
> Joining a team is an excellent idea, but be careful about joining too many too soon. Check out the expectations for members carefully before signing on to be sure you're not overcommitting yourself. And if you do get overwhelmed, scale back on your team memberships.

While all these activities can require a time investment, understand that as you're spending, say, an hour a week on team-related promotional activities to help other sellers, your teammates are doing the same thing to help you. So the power of your 1 hour of activity is worth more like 20 or 40 hours a week, and your shop benefits directly. That's the power of leverage, or of a team—you invest an hour and you get

20 or 40 hours' worth of promotional support from everyone involved. Not a bad use of your time.

An additional benefit of being on a team is being pushed and encouraged creatively. Some teams have weekly project challenges to prod each other to try something new, or to incorporate a particular theme into their work, which also makes for built-in treasury opportunities. For example, your team might have a holiday-related craft challenge to make a Christmas tree ornament or to make a Kwanzaa-inspired table-cloth. Teams help stretch your craftiness while also expanding your marketing reach.

They can keep you entertained, too. Some teams have awards, some collaborate to support a particular cause, and others schedule in-person get-togethers. Being a business owner can be lonely at times, and as a member of a team, you know you always have someone you can whine to, celebrate with, and commiserate with. That may be the biggest reason of all to join a team.

Some teams accept all applicants, and others are *juried*, presumably to control the variety and quality of members.

DEFINITION

Juried teams are made up of members who have had their workmanship and product photography reviewed before being accepted for inclusion on a team, much like an art exhibition. Juried teams are different from open teams in that you have to apply and be accepted.

As a member of a team, your teammates are almost required to help promote your work by including your items in treasuries they create and in social media mentions. If you were to hire a PR firm to do this kind of marketing, it would easily cost you $1,000 a month. So take advantage of your fellow Etsians' help.

You might also want to sign up for the weekly Teams newsletter, which you can subscribe to at etsy.com/mailinglist. Each issue provides news and team promotional opportunities.

Joining Circles

Whereas teams consist of fellow Etsy sellers, circles include Etsy sellers and buyers. To become part of your circle, people simply have to have an Etsy account. To add someone to your circle, bring up their profile page and click **Add to Circle**. It's that simple.

To see who's currently in your circle, click on your name and pull up your public profile. There you'll see how many circles you're currently in on one tab and how many people are in your circle by clicking **Your Circle**. There appears to be a limit of 1,080 people you can include in your circle, although you can join as many other circles as you want.

When someone is in your circle, you can keep up with their activity feed, which is really just a summary of their new Favorites, their new treasury listings, and notifications of when they add people to their own circles. Of course, seeing this information can make you aware of interesting shops and people, too.

Another benefit of being in a circle is that, as with teams, you have that many more people willing to talk you up and praise your work. They're also the people most likely to buy from you or refer your work to others.

While you need to be careful about committing to too many teams, there's no reason to limit the Etsy folks you add to your circle. They may then decide to add you to their circle. If you change your mind later about including someone, you can also easily remove them. Just pull up your circle, scroll to the person you'd like out of your circle, hover over their name, and click on the **X** that appears. Voilà, they're out.

Creating Treasuries

Treasury lists, or treasuries for short, are one of the true gems of Etsy. They're used to both showcase top items on Etsy and encourage fellow Etsy users to get to know each other. It's a win-win for everyone, really.

A treasury is a shopping gallery consisting of 16 Etsy items. An Etsy seller identifies 16 pieces they like that generally have something in common. Maybe they're all brown, display trees, or feature a pearl or a baseball or a little girl. The common thread can be anything the seller desires. A treasury can even be 16 items the person simply liked. The featured pieces are then displayed together in 16 thumbnail images.

Each treasury has the chance to be chosen to be featured on the Etsy home page. Etsy staffers review the treasuries and decide which ones are featured. Treasuries that do make it to the front page suddenly have millions of eyeballs on them, and sellers whose items are included in featured treasures report that such attention can generate additional business opportunities.

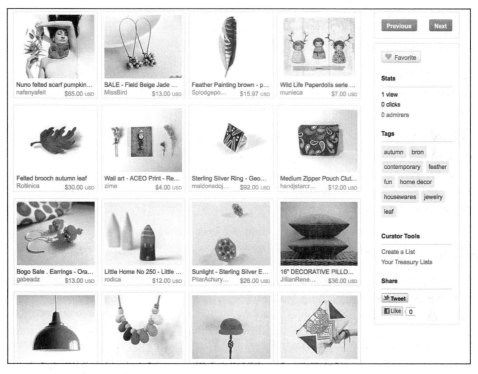

Treasuries are featured on the Etsy home page as well as in Etsy sellers' profiles.

To start a treasury of your own, click **Treasury** on the left side of the Etsy home page. On the next page, you can view existing treasuries or start your own.

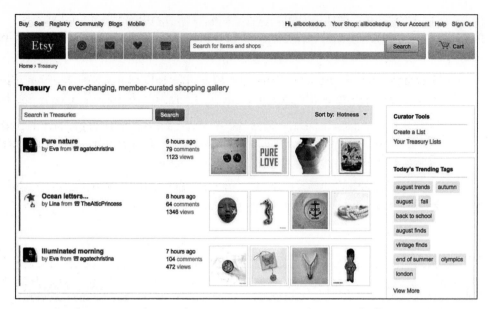

See the most recently created treasuries, or create your own, on the Treasury page.

To make your own treasury, click **Create a List**. (Keep in mind that this is a totally non-self-serving tool—you can't feature any of your own items in a treasury you create.)

The only tricky part, really, of creating a treasury is remembering to note the listing ID number as you review items you like. That's the number you need to have handy as you start creating your treasury. To find an item's listing ID, look in the item's URL. The number that appears after the word *listing* is the listing ID. In this sample listing, the listing ID is 70023186:

> http://www.etsy.com/listing/70023186/floating-pearl-necklace-in-silver-chain

You can paste the whole URL or just the item number in the Listing URL box, but it's probably easier just to paste the whole URL.

Here are some other pieces of information you'll need to prepare a treasure:

> **Title**. This is the name you want to give your Etsy treasury, so it needs to be unique and descriptive, such as NatureLook's recent list, "Keep Calm & Call Mom," or SeleneDream's "Wedding in My Garden." Sure, you can be direct and call it what it is, "Collection of Seashell-Inspired Gifts," but that's not quite as creative.

Description. Next, explain a little about the significance of the listings you've pulled together. Is there a story connecting all the pieces? Something that caught your eye or inspired you?

Privacy. You can choose to make a list visible only to yourself, but that kind of defeats the whole purpose of creating a treasury. Better to make it public.

Tags. Just as buyers find your items through keywords, or tags, they'll find items on your treasury with tags. So use words that describe your complete list as well as tags for individual product categories.

Listing URL. This is where you type, or copy and paste, the URL of the listing you want to feature. Click **OK** to save it.

Etsy makes it easy for you to put together a treasury of listings you like.

If you decide later to edit your list, click the **Edit** button on the right side of the page while looking at your treasury. Then you can edit or remove items.

You can also delete comments others make on your treasury. By placing your mouse over a comment, the **Delete** option will appear and you can click it.

CRAFTY TOOLS

To boost the odds your treasury will be picked to be featured on the Etsy home page, include a wide variety of listings from several different shops that have top-notch product photography.

Expanding Beyond the Etsy Community

If you focus your efforts on promoting your shop and the shops of other equally talented Etsy sellers, odds are very good that new opportunities will come your way. Members of the media, TV producers, writers, and reporters are increasingly turning to Etsy for products to feature in their newspaper and magazine articles, on their TV shows, and in their blogs. The more visible you are on Etsy, the more visible you may become outside Etsy, too.

However, once you've established yourself on Etsy, you may decide to invest some time in actively pursuing attention from the public. People are looking for you on Etsy now, but you can ensure you'll also catch their eye off Etsy.

Offering Coupon Codes and Promo Offers

Advertising a coupon code or special discount may be all you need to catch the eye, and the dollars, of all the extreme couponers and bargain hunters out there. If nothing else, it's very likely you'll have a lot of people checking out your shop—which is what marketing's all about, isn't it?

Coupon codes don't cost you anything until someone buys something. And assuming you built enough profit into your pricing, you're ahead every time someone uses one. That's in contrast to other marketing tactics that cost you money up front, with no guarantee you'll get even one sale.

For more specifics on how to set a coupon code up in your Etsy shop, flip back to Chapter 14.

Issuing Press Releases

If you're most interested in catching the eye of the media, consider writing a press release or tip sheet. In addition to being picked up by newspapers and magazines, press releases may also lead to blog posts, mentions on major news websites, and features in newsletters. You just never really know where a press release will end up, but you can almost be guaranteed that if it's well written, it will be seen by thousands, if not tens or hundreds of thousands of people.

> **CRAFTY TOOLS**
>
> For some guidance in how to structure and write an attention-grabbing press release, check out publicityinsider.com/release.asp.

Press releases are appropriate for alerting the media to news about you and your Etsy shop. For example, your local news may care about the following:

- Impressive sales figures

- New craft techniques you've developed

- Honors and awards you've earned

- New employees you've hired

- National media attention you've received

To get noticed by the national media, you should issue press releases, but you may also need to take more drastic measures, such as sending product samples, which I talk about in a minute.

If you don't have news to report, a better tool to use is the tip sheet, which is a how-to type of document rather than an announcement. Essentially, a tip sheet provides a useful bit of information related to your business, rather than making an announcement, which is what most press releases do. Using the format of a standard press release, you share information, often in list or bulleted form, your reader can use to improve some aspect of their life.

As an Etsy seller, you might share a tip about how to use one of the products you make, such as a hand-knitted wrist warmer. Or perhaps you explain how to tell the difference between cashmere and acrylic fibers. This then gives you the opportunity to weave in a reference to your Etsy shop without being overtly promotional.

You can send your tip sheets to local and national media outlets as long as they're your target audience. That is, *Better Homes and Gardens* may consider your tip sheet on "How to Build a Low-Cost Glass Chandelier," but *Wall Street Banker* or *Podiatry Today* won't. Their readers simply won't care. Think about your audience and their interests as you decide where to send your press releases and tip sheets.

Decide which are your top 10 media outlets—TV stations, magazines, newspapers, radio stations, and bloggers—and send the appropriate editor at each a hand-written cover note with your release. (The "appropriate editor" is the one who generally writes stories in your field, such as lifestyle, food, or home décor.) For the rest of the world, you can use a press release distribution service. Some of the most popular ones include the following:

- Business Wire (businesswire.com)

- PR Newswire (prnewswire.com)

- PRWeb (prweb.com)

- Marketwire (marketwire.com)

There are also free press release distribution sites, although most make the release available online rather than pushing them out to the major media. Mashable published this list of 20 free press release distribution sites a few years ago: mashable.com/2007/10/20/press-releases.

The goal of a press release or tip sheet is to catch the eye of an editor or reporter who may decide to mention you, quote you, or profile you in an upcoming story. Because once you're a media darling, the public will beat a path to your Etsy shop door.

Product Sampling

Because Etsy showcases the best in handmade items, editors and reporters are increasingly turning to Etsy sellers for products to feature in their print, broadcast, and online stories. However, before deciding how to use an item, most editors request a product sample. This is a reasonable request when made by a well-known publication or blogger, so don't be put off by it. If you're asked for a sample, pack it up and ship it off ASAP. The value of having your work shown on the *TODAY Show* or in *Family Circle* is worth tens of thousands of dollars, so don't think twice about it.

If you don't want to wait around for an editor to request a sample, you can also create your own product sampling program. Identify the top media outlets you'd like to have your work be shown in or on, and send a cover letter with a sample of your work to the appropriate editor. You can also send photos of similar pieces, in case that particular pillow or bracelet or wall treatment doesn't strike their fancy.

Pursuing Awards

Another way to attract attention from the media *and* potential buyers is through awards programs. The benefit of winning an award is that forever after, you can refer to yourself as "award-winning." There's value in that.

So which awards should you enter? There are a bunch, in many different categories, so you need to do a little searching to find out all the available competitions in your genre. If you draw in pastel, for example, look for art and drawing competitions. If you make quilts, check for quilting guilds and contest. There's even a plush competition each year, as well as juried craft festivals in towns across America.

Assuming the fee is reasonable, enter as many awards programs you can as long as you feel you have a chance of winning. Each win provides another reason to reach out to the media, in addition to the publicity the competition will garner all on its own.

Everything you do to spread your shop name and glowing reputation can only help build positive buzz among potential customers.

The Least You Need to Know

- Don't miss out on the free tools and networking opportunities Etsy offers.
- As a team member, you gain access to a group of people who are committed to promoting your shop, in exchange for your help in promoting theirs.
- Treasuries are powerful promotional tools, potentially landing your items on the front page of Etsy.
- Sending out press releases and tip sheets can catch the attention of editors who may consider featuring your crafts in their media outlet.
- Enter as many awards programs as you can to gain media exposure, as well as additional reasons to send out your own release or tip sheet.

Making the Most of Social Media

Chapter 16

In This Chapter

- Pinning on Pinterest
- Sharing your work on Facebook
- Tweeting news on Twitter
- Networking on LinkedIn
- Blogging about your baubles
- Staying connected when you're out and about

Today, marketers online and off use social media tools like Facebook, Twitter, LinkedIn, and Pinterest to interact with others and spread news about their company and products. Social media is a great way for Etsy sellers to share information about their creations and keep in touch with buyers and potential customers.

You still want to communicate with your mailing list via email, but also using social media websites gives your product images the chance to go viral.

Many sellers are achieving surprising results through social media, making sales and expanding their customer base more quickly than they thought possible. But although there are several leading social media websites, you might want to start to use just one at first, rather than attempting to master all four at the same time.

In this chapter, I share tips for using social media tools to your—and your Etsy shop's—advantage.

Pinterest

If you need to choose one social media site to focus on, right now it should be Pinterest (pinterest.com). It is the fastest-growing website, with more than 17 million active monthly users as of spring 2012, and that number is only going to get bigger.

Pinterest is like an online bulletin board with virtual pushpins you can use to post and share photos and even videos you like. But it's not like Facebook, where you're sharing family photos at the beach. On Pinterest, you're sharing photos of family room designs you like, evening gowns you like, artwork you like, china and silverware you like—it's a lot like window shopping. And because you're posting images, it's the perfect place for Etsy crafters to be.

On Pinterest, you can view and share beautiful images, including Etsy items you love.

You can pin—meaning upload and share, or link to other already posted—photos of things you love. For your Etsy shop, these could include your latest craft creations, items you custom-made for a client, or shapes that inspire you.

Your goal is to show everyone on Pinterest what you do in the hopes that they'll like and hopefully even repin your photos and show others. And somewhere in there, you might find a customer who will click through and buy what you just shared. In fact, it happens quite a bit, which is why if you have to limit the amount of time you spend on social media, invest it all in Pinterest right now.

Becoming Pinnable

To get started marketing on Pinterest, you have to set up a free account. On the Pinterest home page, simply click the **Join Pinterest** button. You can sign up using your Facebook account, your Twitter account, or your email address.

You'll need to decide whether to create a username that represents your own individual name or your Etsy shop. Given Pinterest's broad usage—from imagining what a renovated kitchen could look like to gathering lots of recipes that call for beets to compiling pictures of your favorite Etsy pieces from your shop and others—you might want to go with using your own name to set up your account. That way, you can help your Etsy buyers get to know more about you through your Pinterest pins and interests, which may help them become even bigger fans of your work.

When your account is active, you'll be given some existing boards—virtual bulletin boards, essentially—to start. If they don't match your interests, just delete them and start new ones. Click on the **Add+** button in the upper right of the Pinterest home page to start a new board.

You may want to have a single board for your Etsy work and others for your other interests, or you can combine them. Here are some ideas for boards:

- Home design or décor
- Real estate
- Gardening
- Retirement
- Travel
- Fashion
- Jewelry
- Recipes
- Wedding ideas
- New baby
- New business
- Cool DIY projects
- Holiday decorating

Or you can create separate boards for the different categories of products you create, much like your shop categories. You might also have a board that shows work in progress, or a board for your workspace, which gives visitors a sense of where and how the magic happens, or a board for your team members, if you have a team of people who support you.

Take a look at the many Etsy sellers who've created Pinterest boards at pinterest. com/etsy to get inspiration for the many types of boards you can create.

CRAFTY TOOLS

You'll notice a lot of white backgrounds on Pinterest, just like on Etsy. If your backgrounds aren't currently white and you'd like to convert them, use FotoFuze (fotofuze.com).

To add your own pieces to your Pinterest board(s), go to your shop and click on a photo of something you'd like to share on a Pinterest board. On the left side of the screen, you'll see several social media buttons, including Pinterest. Click on the **Pinterest** button and then select the board you want to pin your item to.

Any image you pin on Pinterest from Etsy will include a diagonal strip in the top-left corner showing the price of the product. This is one way to let other Pinterest users know the product in that photo is for sale. But even if an image isn't pinned directly from Etsy—say you pull a different angle of a product shot from a blog post you wrote—if you type the **$** and the price, the pin will automatically include the price strip in the upper left when it appears on Pinterest.

Keep in mind that any Etsy listings pinned directly from Etsy automatically display the first product photo you selected for your listing. You can't select a different angle or view, so be sure your first photo is the absolute best.

Strategic Pinning

To start to connect with other Pinterest users, use the **Search** field to find other people who appreciate the same types of products or style as you do. You might search using product names, such as *flower arrangements* or *woven rugs.* Pinterest will show you images that have been tagged with those keywords or phrases on boards other users have created. If the individual's pins are ones you appreciate, you can choose to Follow them, much like on Facebook or Twitter, and Like them, just like on Facebook. That's how you build your Pinterest boards and start creating online connections.

Also let your friends, family, customers, and acquaintances know you're on Pinterest by adding a Pinterest button to your email signature, inserting a link to your Pinterest page in your Etsy shop announcement, tweeting your Pinterest page to your Twitter followers, and using it in a status update as well as in your profile on Facebook. Let everyone know to look for you and your work there.

WATCH OUT!

Although you can certainly pin your own photos of your work, be sure they aren't the only things you pin. Pinterest frowns on users who use the site purely for self-promotion. So also pin photos of fellow Etsians' work, as you do in treasuries.

The key to success on Pinterest is getting people to repin your images on their boards. To encourage that, you may want to hold a contest. Ask your followers to repin your images, with the individual who repins the most in the next, say, 24 hours, or 3 days, wins a prize. The prize could be a custom-made piece from your shop or something else, like an Amazon gift card.

Then keep adding new images as you add items to your Etsy shop, pinning them to the appropriate board. If you can add at least one new image each week on Pinterest, you're in good shape; if you can add more, you'll be even better off. And don't forget to follow other Etsy buyers and sellers who have similar interests and taste as yours.

For more ideas about how to market your Etsy shop, or any business, using Pinterest, check out this great article on Copyblogger: copyblogger.com/pinterest-marketing.

Facebook

Another major player in the social media space is Facebook (facebook.com). About 526 million active daily users, as of March 2012, from all around the world use Facebook to connect and reconnect with friends, family, colleagues, childhood pals—you name it. Where Pinterest is all about photos and images, Facebook is more about newsy updates and personal photos. It's more of a global water cooler, where people check in, say hello, and then get back to whatever they were doing.

Facebook connects you to people you might never have the chance to interact with in your everyday life, such as friends who live out of town, colleagues in other cities, and family members in other parts of the world.

Setting up a personal Facebook page is simple as long as you have an email address. Then you can add a photo of yourself (which you can change at any time), a brief profile, and places to find you online.

Of course, you'll want to mention you're an Etsy seller and have a link to your Etsy shop front and center on your profile. So even if someone randomly comes across your page, they may be curious enough to go see what you make and sell. That's exactly what you want—people checking out your crafts!

Making Personal Connections

Folks who are on Facebook are pretty active, generally checking in daily to read others' status updates and look at posted photos. To get the most out of Facebook and the connections you make, you'll want to log in at least daily, too.

You should also look to connect with people you know, such as fellow Etsy sellers on your teams or in your circles, fellow crafters, customers, and friends who support your work. You can find them by using the **Search** bar at the top of the page. Not everyone is on Facebook, however, so it's possible you won't find some people.

As your list of Facebook friends grows, so does your marketing team. Your Facebook friends are the people most likely to comment on and share what you post, just like Pinterest users repin photos they like.

To start, you may just want to lurk, or read everyone else's status updates, without typing anything yourself. That's okay at first, but the sooner you start sharing information about yourself and your crafts and becoming part of the Facebook community, the better. Here are some ideas for Facebook status updates:

- Comments on what you're working on and how it's going

- Posts indicating when you get a great idea for a new craft project

- Information about a custom order you just received

- Excitement about a sale you just made, including a photo from the piece that was sold

- An announcement about your latest piece, along with a photo of the listing

- Comments about a craft-related trip you just returned from and what you enjoyed most

- Posts expressing frustration with a particular part of the artistic process

- Requests for feedback or input regarding a great idea you just had

Facebook is meant to foster engagement, or a two-way dialogue with your friends and acquaintances. It's not just for announcements, but for conversations and discussions. So as you're posting updates, first ask yourself whether what you're going to tell people helps others get to know you better and if it could be of interest to your ideal customer. If not, don't bother typing it. (Hint: If you're about to tell us what you had for lunch or that you're headed to the post office, skip it.)

Creating a Facebook Business Page

There are actually two types of Facebook pages you can create: a personal page, which I just talked about, and a page for your business, which used to be called a fan page. To set up one a business page, click the **Create a Page** link at the very bottom of any Facebook page.

Whereas your personal Facebook page was designed to help you connect, or reconnect, with friends and family who are interested in what's going on in your life, a Facebook business page, called a *fan page*, should be devoted to your Etsy shop. Here you can share the joys and frustrations of crafting, show photos of pieces in progress, ask for feedback or direction from your fans and customers, and keep them posted regarding exciting events and achievements. You can build a community of fans here on your Facebook fan page by sharing business information only.

On the next page, click **Pages** in the left navigation bar. That will take you to another page that has **Create a Page+** in the upper right. That is the first real step in creating a separate page for your Etsy shop.

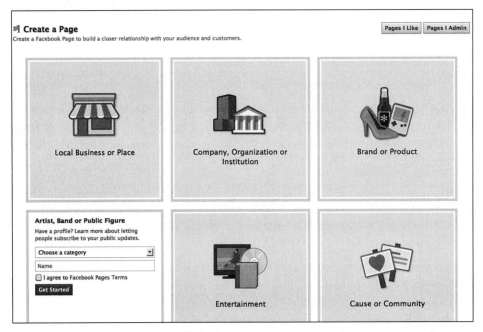

Facebook Pages are specifically for businesses, organizations, brands, causes, and events, rather than individuals.

After creating your business page, you can start using it to market your Etsy shop. You can add an image to run across the top, much like on an Etsy shop banner, as well as a brief description of your business and a link to your shop.

But just like on your personal Facebook page, don't set up your business page and let it lie dormant. Come back to it often, and share news and information related to your Etsy shop that might entice your fans to go and check out what you've been working on.

In addition to product photos and updates, you can also alert fans—who are your friends, customers, prospects, family, and fellow Etsians—to upcoming craft fairs or juried shows you'll be participating in, magazine or newspaper articles you were mentioned in, awards you received, new craft techniques you perfected or tried for the first time, as well as special offers and promotions you have for people who like your work.

CRAFTY TOOLS

You can share that Etsy coupon code you created for your Etsy shop customers with your Facebook fans, or you can create special Facebook codes that allow you to track and compare which site brings you more business.

Twitter

Twitter (twitter.com) is a microblogging service that allows you to share information, much like Facebook's status updates, as long they're 140 characters or less. You have to be concise on Twitter. And that is part of its appeal—text messages on Twitter don't have to be in-depth.

However, unlike Pinterest and Facebook, with Twitter, you can't directly tweet photos (although you can insert links to photos in your tweets), which makes it a little less appealing, but it's still useful for Etsy sellers. Letters and words are how you communicate with your Twitter followers.

You have to get to the point quickly on Twitter. You only have 140 characters per tweet to express yourself.

After setting up your new Twitter account, which takes an email address, you should first write your bio and upload a photo of yourself. Then start following people. These are people you want to hear from via Twitter so you might search for and follow other Etsy sellers, artists you admire, friends, family, local businesspeople—whoever you want. In turn, many of those people will follow you back, meaning they're now signed up to automatically receive your tweets when you send them out.

Next, start tweeting, talking about your Etsy business or a project you're working on that others might like to hear about. Humor is always appreciated and can make you memorable.

Regular Tweeting Is Key

Although Twitter updates are required to be short, most Twitter users make up for that in frequency of posts. Many post multiple times a day.

One way they do that regularly is by retweeting, or resending someone else's message with a personal comment attached. So although you might not have anything to report today, it's perfectly acceptable—even encouraged—to monitor what your followers are saying and then retweet it to your Twitter followers.

> **CRAFTY TOOLS**
>
> You can connect your Etsy shop to Facebook and Twitter with one click. So every time you make something an Etsy Favorite, it will appear on your Facebook and Twitter pages. Go to **Settings** under **Your Account** and click **Connect with Twitter** and/or **Connect with Facebook**.

Although you can't directly attach or embed an image in a tweet, you can insert a link to a photo, such as an Etsy page, or to your Etsy shop. To share a photo with your followers, you can either click on the camera icon under the Twitter status bar on your computer screen and identify the photo you want shown, or you can use an app like TwitPic, which allows you to take a photo live, add a comment, and share. The photo is shared as a link.

Photos are most effective when preceded by a comment to put them in context, such as, "Just listed my latest creation. So excited. bit.ly/1234." This is only 56 characters, which is good because it allows space up front for your friends to retweet it and add their own note. If they did, it could read something like, "My friend's gorgeous knitting RT @knitstar Just listed my latest creation. So excited. bit.ly/1234." That tweet is 99 characters and includes your Twitter account name, which I made up (knitstar). Or maybe, "Love this! RT @knitstar Just listed my latest creation. So excited. bit.ly/1234." Of course, the web link would lead to your Etsy listing. (Bitly.com is one of the most popular websites for shortening long URLs.)

Creating a Tweet Schedule

Because the key to Twitter success is frequency of posts, many users batch their posts. That is, they'll write several at once and then schedule them to go out throughout the day, or over the next couple days. You can't do this directly on Twitter, but you can use one of several smartphone apps to accomplish this. One of the most popular is TweetDeck (tweetdeck.com). Just click **Schedule Tweets** in the right navigation bar, type in your messages, and schedule when you'd like them to go out. Simple as that.

Another tweet scheduling app is Buffer (bufferapp.com), which you can also use in conjunction with Tweriod (tweriod.com), to know when the best time is for you to tweet to your fans and customers based on when they're on Twitter.

CRAFTY TOOLS

Hashtags are perhaps Twitter's greatest gift to social media. When you comment on something you want others to spot, you can add a hashtag (#) followed by a keyword at the end of your tweet. This makes it easy to search Twitter for these discussions. For example, **#etsy** adds your tweet to the Etsy discussion and makes it searchable.

The goal with Twitter is to post frequently on your area of expertise—your awesome crafting skills—and to continually add to your list of followers. Ideally, each one of your followers is a potential customer, although you won't really know that unless they all buy from you. So keep following people you come across who are potential customers, industry influencers, or interesting people you want to get to know.

LinkedIn

Considered more of a professional networking tool than water cooler, LinkedIn is used by executives and head hunters more than crafters, but that doesn't mean it can't help you build your Etsy business.

Known as more of a site for professionals and white-collar workers, LinkedIn helps get you in front of folks who may have a little more disposable income than most.

You can get a LinkedIn account for free, although they also offer a premium version that costs about $20 a month. You don't need that to start, so just register for an account and set up your profile by uploading your photo and typing in a brief bio that mentions Etsy.

Posting

Whereas Facebook and Twitter are big on regular status updates, LinkedIn is more about targeted networking. Yes, you should provide status updates that will be of interest to a professional crew, such as the latest Etsy usage stats, but there's less of an emphasis on sharing a blow-by-blow of your day here.

You can also link your Facebook and Twitter accounts to your LinkedIn account so that when you post on either of the other sites, it will automatically be imported to your LinkedIn page. Assuming you're keeping your posts business-related, this is a good idea and will take the pressure off to come up with yet another status update.

Joining Groups

One thing LinkedIn has that can be very helpful are its groups. Like Etsy Teams, groups are what they sound like—people with similar interests or industries or jobs.

You can find groups you may want to join by looking at LinkedIn's suggestions for you, which are under the **Groups** tab at the top of the page, or do a search for keywords in the Groups Directory. *Etsy* would be an obvious choice, as well as terms related to the medium you work in or target buyers.

You might need to apply to be accepted into a group, which may take a day, but then you'll start to receive email updates regarding discussions occurring among group members. You can join in and share your perspective, read what others have to say, or even start your own discussion.

Becoming part of any community of like-minded crafters is almost always a good idea, so look for similar groups on LinkedIn.

Answering Questions

Another interesting and useful feature LinkedIn offers is Answers. Under the **More** tab at the top of the page, you'll see **Answers** at the top of the pop-up window. When you click on it, you'll be taken to a long list of questions fellow LinkedIn members have asked. Answers is your opportunity to share your expertise with others and, in doing so, gain some credibility and perhaps some followers.

Responding to questions other LinkedIn members have asked will likely earn you respect and maybe a few potential customers.

You can also ask your own question here, too, keeping in mind your audience. Questions about managing a business, finding suppliers, expanding, and other business-related questions would be completely appropriate here. But queries about craft technique and Etsy policies would not, mainly because few LinkedIn members may be qualified to respond. Head back to Etsy for that kind of advice.

Your Blog

The social media tools I've been talking about so far have their own style, format, and guidelines. Blogs, however, are much more freeform. A blog is really just a personal journal you can devote to business or artistic purposes, if you so choose. But the point is to create a space online where you can share words and images with people who are interested in your work.

One popular blogging tool is WordPress (wordpress.com). With WordPress, you can create a blog that can also be used as a full website, with pages for ecommerce (sales of your crafts), video, resources, and more. The benefit of WordPress, and its equally popular cousin Blogger (blogger.com), is that both are free. Be aware, however, that Blogger's terms of service demand that any content you create at the site becomes the property of Blogger; for that reason, many people are moving their blogs to WordPress.

WordPress has emerged as the most popular free blog-building platform because of its ease of use.

A Free Self-Promotion Tool

Blogging is an effective online promotional tool because you control how the page is laid out, what message you present, and the images you share. There are no limits on the number or words or characters you can use, nor are you prohibited from actively selling your pieces on your blog. The only downside is that you may need a little help setting up your pages.

If you'd like some step-by-step guidance in setting up a blog, a number of videos are available online for that very purpose. This is one of the more-watched videos: youtube.com/watch?v=MWYi4_COZMU. If you're considering setting up your own self-hosted WordPress blog on wordpress.*org*, which has many more features and benefits than wordpress.*com*, take a look at this informative video by Michael Hyatt: michaelhyatt.com/ez-wordpress-setup.html.

Once you set up your blog, you'll want to redirect it to a URL you've chosen and registered at a domain registration site, such as GoDaddy.com. Choose a blog name that reflects your business, which can be your Etsy shop name, too, and then follow the WordPress instructions to link your blog (which has a *name*.wordpress.com address) to your new domain (which looks something like cuteetsystuff.com).

> **CRAFTY TOOLS**
>
> Many Etsy sellers have their own blogs and have even joined the Etsy WordPress blogs team. If you're just setting up your own blog, this could be an excellent team to become part of. Check out etsy.com/teams/9494/wordpress-blogs to learn more.

The challenge with blogging is very similar to the challenge with any other social media sites—committing the time to frequently communicate with your followers. Once you start regularly posting 300- to 500-word articles on your blog, people will start to read them. People who like them and want to be alerted when you post a new article will subscribe using an RSS feed. (Do a Google search to learn more about setting that up.)

On your blog, you can regularly post pictures of your latest creations, along with commentary about them or explanations of how you made them. You can talk about the latest news in the Etsy world, or in your particular crafting genre, or even in your backyard. You can share as much personal information about yourself as you feel comfortable, understanding that showing a little personality and giving readers a sense of who you are almost always has a positive impact on sales.

Leveraging Your Blog

Your blog can be your central marketing tool, if you let it. If you start with a blog and devote time and energy to keeping it updated, you can then design a social media campaign around it. For example, you can tweet about your latest blog post and include a link to it. You can pin an image of your latest piece, which you just blogged about, as well as posting a Facebook status update with a link to your blog and a photo. You can also shoot a short video in which you demonstrate some aspect of your creative process.

One of the best things about having a blog is that you can monitor how many people you're reaching each week or each month. Monitoring your WordPress stats, you can see how many people are reading your posts and which posts are most popular. Use this information to decide what to write about in the future.

As a blogger, you should reach out to other craft-related blogs and offer to write a guest post. You can share information about what you do with people who aren't yet reading your blog and perhaps entice them to start following you. Until you're blogging, however, you won't be taken seriously if you offered to write a guest post, nor would it be very useful because your end goal is to attract people back to your blog.

You can also use your blog as a revenue generator, accepting ads on it for pay, or you can design and feature your own ads to promote your Etsy work. You own and control your blog, so you can do just about anything, as long as it's legal, to promote yourself.

Making Mobile Connections

The rising popularity of smartphones and the new capabilities they provide has created new opportunities for Etsy sellers, and it's even more important to be connected to your Etsy shop when you're on the go. That means downloading these social media apps for your iPhone or Android so they're always at your fingertips.

Facebook, Twitter, LinkedIn, and Pinterest all have mobile apps that make it much quicker and easier to stay in touch. Instead of having to log into the world wide web and type in a site's URL, you can simply tap on the mobile app icon on your smartphone. This accessibility means that even more people will be watching your Facebook updates, reading your tweets, checking out your LinkedIn updates, and viewing your Pinterest images. Don't miss out. Download those apps now, for free.

Even more important, download Etsy's mobile app so you can immediately monitor your sales activity, curate treasuries on the fly, and stay in touch with potential buyers when you're not at your desktop.

With everyone connected 24/7, customers and fans expect almost immediate responses. Don't disappoint them. Download the Etsy app for free and stay in touch.

The Least You Need to Know

- Pinterest is like an online bulletin board onto which you can pin photos, including your Etsy listings.
- Facebook is the perfect place to tell your friends about your latest creation, or to ask for feedback regarding which materials your followers think will be more popular.

- Use Twitter to share news of your current project and include a link to a photo of your latest work.

- Most people consider LinkedIn a professional networking site, but that doesn't mean you can't share information about your Etsy business there.

- A blog is the least restrictive social media tool; build your social media strategy around your blog posts, and you'll have plenty of content to share.

- Smartphone apps enable you to stay connected with all the social media sites, as well as your own Etsy shop, while you're away from your computer.

Cultivating Repeat Buyers

In This Chapter

- Setting the stage for a purchase
- Using the right communication style
- Follow-up fundamentals
- Asking for (positive) feedback

You already know repeat buyers are much more profitable than one-time sales, which is why doing all you can to foster long-term customer relationships makes a lot of sense. However, the work required to establish and nurture customer relationships starts even before you make a sale and continues long after you've shipped the purchase.

The way you communicate with Etsy buyers, including the language and tone you use in your Etsy shop, the manner in which you answer questions through Etsy conversations, the types of thank you notes you enclose with orders, and any follow-up emails you exchange with buyers—even unhappy ones—all determine how satisfied your customers are and how many ultimately come back to buy from you again. If you take the time to show how dedicated to customer satisfaction you are right from the get-go, you'll attract more buyers and you'll hold onto them longer.

In this chapter, I explain how to leverage your first sale to generate additional sales and positive feedback that encourages others to buy, too. Follow up and regular communication are key.

After-the-Sale Customer Service

Your opportunity to really impress buyers happens as soon as they click Add to Cart because that's when they officially become your customer. That's also when you need to stay in touch as much as possible, demonstrating ongoing customer service.

Really, there's no such thing as too much communication at this stage. A customer has just paid you money, and they may be a little nervous about whether the item they receive will match the description, whether it will arrive in time to give as a birthday gift next weekend, whether it will arrive in one piece—you get the picture. They're nervous. Fortunately, you can turn that anxiety into excitement and anticipation simply through regular email communication.

Keeping in Touch

By staying in close contact with customers until, and after, their package arrives, you're virtually holding their hand, reassuring them that you're a reputable seller and that if, by some fluke, they're not happy with their order, you'll make things right. Or if it arrives damaged, you'll ship them another one. Each follow-up email you send makes them feel more and more confident and happy about their choice. That's the essence of customer service—ensuring your customer is informed and knows exactly what to expect.

If you're not sure when you should be in touch, here are some suggestions:

To thank them for their purchase. As soon as you receive a sold notification, send your customer a note to thank them for doing business with you and let them know you're carefully packing their purchase for shipment.

When you ship the package. Use the Etsy Shipping Notifications Tool to let your customer know exactly when you mailed their package and provide tracking information so they can monitor its journey to them. When you mark an item as shipped, click on the Shipping Notification to send this information to the buyer.

After you ship the package. While the shipment is en route, send a quick follow-up email thanking the buyer again for their purchase, passing along an expected delivery date (which the shipper gives you), and offer to answer any questions or concerns once it arrives, and then give them your private email address.

Once it arrives. You can never say "thank you" too many times, and this is another opportunity. You can also ask for feedback at this point or ask if they would like to be added to your mailing list to be updated on promotions and new items. You might even consider doing a survey using SurveyMonkey to assess how well you're satisfying your customers, or to get ideas for crafts they'd like but haven't been able to find on Etsy.

Creating a system for regular communication, along with standard messages, ensures these emails won't take much of your time but will significantly increase your odds of completely satisfying your buyers.

Buyers from Courtney Gifford's Lovebugs shop (etsy.com/shop/lovebuggz) are clearly satisfied with her hand-stamped jewelry because at least 50 percent of her customers are repeats. In fact, one customer has bought from her five times in the last couple years she's had an Etsy shop. Keeping her prices low starts the transaction on the right foot. Courtney ships her pieces in an organza bag set inside a simple brown box, which has won her praise. She ensures her customers are pleased with their purchases so that when they have another gift-giving occasion, they may think of her.

Providing Regular Follow-Up

Communicating during the purchase and shipping process helps endear you to your buyers, which is good. You always want your customers to think highly of you. But you also want them to buy more from you, and to encourage that, you need to stay at the top of their mind. That means simply reminding them that you exist and that your Etsy shop has great handmade crafts for sale.

CRAFTY TOOLS

To give Etsy shoppers a reason to give you their email address, hold a weekly or monthly drawing for a free item from your shop for anyone who signs up for your mailing list. Then promote this contest heavily, such as in your Shop Announcements, product descriptions, packing lists, Etsy conversations with potential buyers, in your email signature, and on all your social media outlets.

Although you can't market to buyers who haven't given you their email address or signed up for your mailing list, you can certainly keep in touch with those who have.

Here are some reasons to get back in touch:

- To offer a thank you coupon code for a second (or third, or fourth) purchase

- To announce a new product line or category you think they might be interested in

- To ask for suggestions regarding products they might be interested in buying

- To announce a contest or competition

- To let them know when you're in their local area

Don't inundate folks on your mailing list with a barrage of emails, but an email every 1 or 2 weeks helps remind them of your existence so that when they think of something they'd like to have or give, they'll turn to you first.

Managing Buyer Feedback

Of course, while you're doing your best to talk to customers, once in a while, they'll talk back. Most of the time the messages are flattering and complementary, but you will get complaints here and there. Some will be legitimate, especially if you made an error in how you described your piece or took too long to ship it. Others will just be complainers or people looking for a reason to request a refund.

It's hard to know what kind of person you're dealing with at the outset, so it's best to assume each person has a legitimate complaint.

Requesting Input

However, the fact that a buyer took the time to get in touch is good news. No, really. Even if they're writing to complain, you've just been given a chance to learn how to improve your shop. Bill Gates has been quoted as saying, "Your most unhappy customers are your greatest source of learning." So the more you hear from your customers, the more you can strengthen your bond with them and learn how to better satisfy them.

Some buyers will get in touch via Etsy conversations, others may email you if they have your address, and others may simply give you feedback as a way to let you know how you did as a seller. Take it all as useful input—some will be more useful than others.

Any customer input is useful, even if all they tell you is, "Great job." But to let customers know they have a way to rate your shop's performance, you might consider encouraging them to give feedback. Ask them for it.

You could even send a follow-up email asking for feedback. To explain how to do that, suggest buyers go to **Your Account** and click the **Feedback** link. There, they can leave feedback for their purchases. You can also leave feedback for your buyers here. Feedback is one way Etsy helps identify legitimate, quality buyers and sellers—people who won't waste your time or frequently ask for refunds. Feedback is one indication of whether someone is a customer you want or not.

Your request could come shortly after you ship a package, or a few days later, after it arrives. You could say something like:

> If you have any questions about your purchase, feel free to email me at [*your email*]. I would also really appreciate it if you'd have a minute to give me some feedback on Etsy. What did I do well, and what could I have done better?

Not all buyers will take the time to give you feedback, so pay special attention to the ones who do.

Stay on top of feedback you need to leave for your purchases as well as feedback your shop has received.

Dealing with Negative Comments

No matter how hard you try, at some point you will come across a dissatisfied customer. Expect it, so when it happens you won't feel so disheartened. It's coming.

When you receive negative feedback from a customer, you can choose to leave the situation alone, or you can try to make it right. The upside of offering to do something to satisfy the customer is twofold: you may convert that customer from unhappy to extremely loyal (that's common when a problem is resolved) *and* if you can satisfy them, you can request that they change their feedback to positive.

Unlike on eBay, where feedback cannot be changed (sellers can only respond to buyer comments), Etsy allows buyers and sellers to mutually agree to change a negative or neutral rating. It's called Kiss and Make Up, and this link appears under any negative feedback you've given as a buyer. Under **Your Account**, click **Feedback**, and look at the **Completed Feedback**.

Buyers and sellers can agree to change negative feedback to positive after a situation has been corrected or resolved.

Aiming to maintain a 90+ positive feedback is a smart goal because the lower your feedback score, the more nervous buyers will be about buying from you. So when you receive negative feedback, it really is in your best long-term interest to try to convince your buyer to change it. There are limits, however, to what you should be willing to do.

If you made an error of some kind, definitely do what you can to correct the situation and make the buyer happy. You really do owe them.

If you're not sure whose error it is, it's still in your best interest to see what you can do to correct the problem. Maybe the customer thought they had ordered the blue scarf and mistakenly clicked the Add to Cart button on the orange scarf listing. Is that your fault? No. But the end result is that they're not happy and they're going to tell all their friends how unhappy they are. So why not offer to swap the blue scarf for the orange, and throw in an especially nice bonus for their inconvenience?

And when it's clearly the buyer's fault, it's still wise to see what you can do to turn their frown upside down. This is so much easier to do when the buyer can admit his or her mistake, but even if they can't blame anyone other than you, why not see how you can make them happy? It really is worth money to convert them from a dissatisfied customer to a satisfied one.

Those customers who leave negative feedback can frequently be turned into your best customers if you go the extra mile to make them happy. That's how you build a huge customer base.

The Least You Need to Know

- Communication is the key to keeping customers happy.
- Before you start emailing customers regularly, however, get their permission. Maybe even give them an incentive to join your mailing list.
- Buyers won't always leave you feedback automatically, especially if they're happy with their order. When they're not happy, you'll hear right away.
- Do all you can, within reason, to convert an unhappy customer into a happy one to keep your feedback score above 90 percent positive and to demonstrate your commitment to customer satisfaction.
- Dissatisfied customers who have their issues resolved to their satisfaction frequently become your best, most loyal buyers.

Growing Your Business

5

Although Etsy can be a business unto itself, providing you with a sizeable income, many Etsy sellers have found that it's an even better door-opener. Once on Etsy, many crafters have been discovered by interior designers, art galleries, magazines, and bloggers interested in featuring their work. Etsy can be a stepping-stone to even bigger and better creative opportunities.

But don't overlook great opportunities on Etsy to be promoted and to promote fellow Etsians. Joining teams of sellers and circles of like-minded creative pros can boost your shop's visibility and forge important relationships with other crafters—crafters with connections.

Etsy can be the start of your creative career or the basis of a thriving craft business—you get to choose.

Where to Turn for Support

Chapter 18

In This Chapter

- Identifying your biggest business challenges
- Finding outside support
- Tapping into Etsy resources
- Delegating some of your work

Anyone who thinks success on Etsy comes automatically—that all a crafter needs to do is register at the site, list some crafts, and sit back and make money—will be sorely disappointed. Sure, Etsy is a terrific marketplace and the top venue for connecting with buyers who value handmade products, but that doesn't mean selling is easy. In fact, it rarely is.

Creating quality, desirable products is only the first step in setting up and managing a profitable Etsy store. Several other factors also come into play. Fortunately, Etsy is one of the most collaborative, helpful communities of business owners around.

In this chapter, I explain where you can turn when you have questions about Etsy or need help with some aspect of your Etsy business. Many resources are available to assist you, and this chapter introduces several.

Overcoming Etsy Challenges

Etsy has worked hard to create a website that's easy to use, easy to navigate, and provides a helping hand whenever possible, but some Etsy sellers encounter challenges that have little or nothing to do with Etsy itself.

Some of those challenges include the following:

>   **Managing the workload.** Whether you're a full-time or part-time Etsy seller, getting the work done can be difficult at times as other priorities emerge.

>   **Product pricing.** Being able to sell your creations for more than it cost you to make them, including a fee for your time, can also be a struggle at first.

>   **Cash flow.** In addition to ensuring you're not losing money on each sale, you also need to be sure you have enough money coming in to cover the cost of supplies for your next project.

>   **Making time for marketing.** If you're busy enough with orders to be really busy for a stretch, it's likely you won't have time to market your shop—yet that's the key to future sales.

>   **Fulfillment.** Packing and shipping orders is easy when you only have a few to prep, but if you get a rush of sales, getting those purchases out can be a challenge.

>   **Self-discipline.** As you shift from a crafter or hobbyist to a business owner, being disciplined enough to turn off the TV and work on another listing or staying up late to finish a custom order is important. Only you can make yourself do what needs to be done.

>   **Jack-of-all-trades.** You're a talented crafter, but you might not know anything about money, or marketing, or shipping. Yet you need to have that knowledge to stay in business.

The good news is you're surrounded by people and tools that can fill in any gaps you have in your knowledge or experience. And Etsy is the best place to start.

Teaming Up with Teams

One of the best places to connect with like-minded sellers is through Etsy's Teams, which are groups of members who have banded together for a common goal. You can find a complete list of all the Etsy teams by clicking **Community** on the home page and then clicking **Teams**.

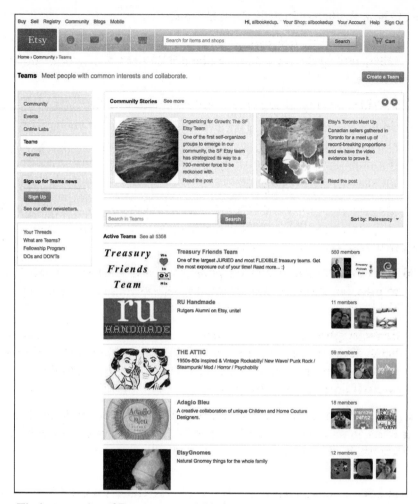

The huge number of Etsy teams available for you to join makes it rather unlikely you'll be unable to find your place within the community.

There are currently more than 5,300 Etsy teams, some of which are organized around geography, some around a common handmade product, some around a cause. Etsy puts no restrictions on why a team exists. One of the few rules is that each team has to have at least one captain and that Etsy takes no responsibility for a team's actions or activities.

CRAFTY TOOLS

Starting your own team is easy, and you'll automatically be the captain if you take charge and set one up. For step-by-step instructions, check out etsy.com/help/article/344. You can then invite people you know to join, to put together your own Etsy dream team.

So if you're a seamstress or crafter with extra fabric, you might want to join the This for That Fabric Traders team. If you're of Latin American descent, you might want to consider joining that team. Or the EtsyNewComers team might be for you if you're just getting up to speed on selling on Etsy.

To find teams to join, search on the Teams page for keywords related to your interests, the city you live in, the type of work you create, or some other commonality you're fascinated with.

Some teams are open, meaning all you need to do to join is click **Join this Team** to become part of it. Voilà! You're in. Read the description of the group in the upper right of the team page to find out if you can simply sign up or if you need to be invited.

Other groups are closed and require an invitation or an application to be considered for membership. For example, the anyone can apply to join the Sparkle Girls team, and as part of the application, the team considers the following:

> Applicants with a minimum of 10 Etsy listings and 5 sales may apply. Feedback ratings are taken into consideration when making the decision regarding acceptance. Shops must sell handmade products for girls or boutique supplies.

The team description can help you make a decision regarding your fit with the team. In this example, if you lack sufficient listings or don't sell products for girls, you know this team isn't a good fit for your Etsy business. Fortunately, you have nearly 5,400 others from which to choose.

Once you're part of a team, you can use your new teammates as advisers, turning to them for feedback on new ideas, guidance on how to handle certain situations, and encouragement when you're having a bad day.

Many teams have weekly promotional challenges or require members to create a new treasury each week, while others are less demanding. Of course, demanding can be an extremely helpful thing if you lack self-discipline or need a little push to set aside time to work on your Etsy shop.

Finding Help on Forums

Each Etsy Team has its own forum to facilitate discussions among members. Only members can post and respond, although members can also choose whether to make the discussion public or private. Be sure you check to see which it is, public or private, before you post oh-so-helpful insider tips that could weaken your competitive advantage if they were made public.

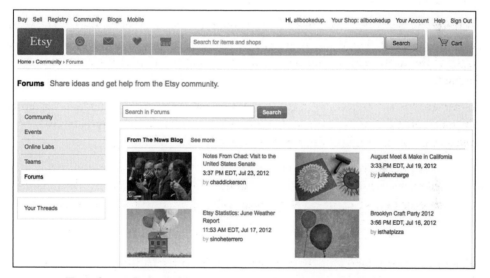

Team forums look just like a regular Etsy forum; the only difference is the individuals who have access and permission to see and comment on posts.

Team forums are different from the general Etsy member forum, which is public and everyone on Etsy can participate in. But because your team consists of other individuals with something in common, it's likely the information shared within a team will be more specific to your situation, and perhaps more helpful.

If you're nervous about asking a question in a potentially public forum, you can also reach out and contact an Etsy member on your team directly. As a fellow team member, it's likely they'll be willing to help you out if they can. Etsians are like that.

Catching Up with the Etsy Blog

Etsy Teams are probably your best bet for selling information and commiseration, but the Etsy blog is an excellent source of up-to-date news about all things Etsy. By clicking **Blogs** and then choosing **Etsy News** from the drop-down menu, you can read about the month's hottest styles, upcoming online and in-person events, updates about the Etsy site, and in-depth reports on topics related to DIY projects and crafting.

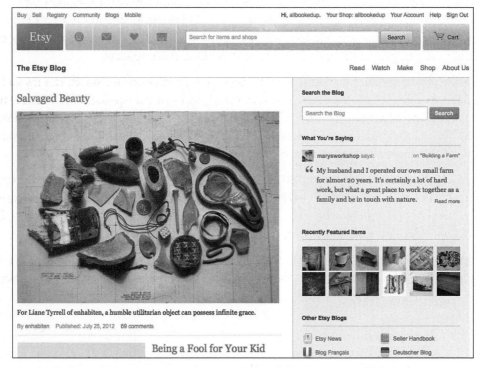

The best source for news about Etsy's present and future is the Etsy blog, which is updated regularly with information useful for Etsy sellers.

CRAFTY TOOLS

Etsy's Online Labs is another great resource, which you can find by clicking **Community** on the home page and choosing **Online Labs** from the drop-down list. Here you can watch archived video programs about successful selling on Etsy or demonstrating a particular artistic technique. To find upcoming web events, just click on the **Events** tab on the left side of the Etsy home page.

Whether you're interested in learning more about successful selling on Etsy or you don't want to miss an upcoming video presentation, the Etsy blog should be your starting point.

Checking Out Special Reports

Within the Etsy blog, alongside short newsy notes about Etsy the company, are reports researched, written, and produced to help you be more successful on Etsy. If you're looking for a guide to what's currently selling on Etsy and what the gurus expect to sell next month, you'll want to download these reports.

In the monthly Merchandising Report, on top of predictions for which shapes and colors and products are going to be hot, you'll find general tips for steps you can take to sell more. Some will be reminders, such as retaking photos that don't adequately showcase your pieces or retagging items with new keywords, and others will be new tools and sites you need to become familiar with.

In the Etsy Statistics report, you'll get a snapshot of how Etsy did last month overall, to spot sales trends you may want to take advantage of. These reports are more useful for longer-term sellers, who have a sales history they can refer to for comparison, but watching the trends can help you evaluate your own shop's results, too.

Few other websites take the time to provide this level of information and support. It's worth your while to study it and see what the stats can mean for you and your shop.

Etsy News Blog

Etsy Statistics: June Weather Report

Story by sinohetarrero
Published on July 17, 2012 in Company News
Photo by Libertad Leal

June brought sunny skies and long summer days to Brooklyn, just in time for Etsy's seventh birthday. It was a month filled with all the good things: beach time, summer reading, refreshing snacks (watermelon, anyone?) and backyard barbeques. The Etsy community had reason to celebrate as well, growing in members and goods sold compared to June 2011.

The stats:

- $61.9 million of goods (after refunds and cancellations) were sold by our community in June, 6.1% lower than May's $65.9 million
- That represents 2,951,224 items sold for the month, 2.7% lower than May's 3,034,442
- 2,184,850 new items were listed in the month, 2.8% lower than May's 2,248,143
- 689,614 new members joined the Etsy community in the month, up 1,249, or 0.2%, from May
- 1.23 billion page views were recorded on the site in June

The $61.9 million of goods sold (after refunds and cancellations) represents a 65.1% increase from June 2011's total. At the same time, items sold were up 54.3%.

The Etsy Statistics: Weather Report provides a snapshot of how the company's sales are trending overall, so you can compare your sales and see if you're missing out on opportunities or are right there with the pack.

Getting Work Done

Knowing where to turn for support in building your Etsy business will make it possible for you to do just that—build it. But in many cases, you simply might not know how to handle certain aspects of managing your business. Maybe you can churn out hand-blown glass Christmas ornaments quickly but can't seem to tackle your bookkeeping. Or you can make book sculptures easily but have no idea how to set up a website.

The good news is that the core of your business is based on what you make, so as long as you're good at that and have demand for what you create, the rest you can figure out. In fact, you don't personally need to know how to do everything in your business—you just need to surround yourself with experts who can do it for you.

Hiring Independent Contractors

You might be thinking you need to hire employees, but you don't. You should put off hiring employees as long as possible—until you're paying more in fees to independent contractors than you would pay a part-time or full-time employee.

When you engage an independent contractor to complete a task for you, the advantage is that you both agree to the scope of the project, such as packing and mailing 40 boxes to customers, and on the payment, maybe $10 an hour. When the work is done and you've paid the agreed-upon fee, you have no future commitment to your helper. You can decide to hire him or her again when you need some supplemental help ... or not. But you'll only pay for their services when you want.

If you hire an employee, you'll pay their salary or hourly wages each week, whether you have enough work to fill their time or not. That's the downside, which is why hiring an employee isn't a good idea until you have a consistent cash flow coming in and an ongoing need for support.

Independent contractor is a generic term for someone who agrees to work for you without an ongoing employment commitment. By the same token, you're not their only client—independent contractors have the freedom to work with as many clients as they like. This is the disadvantage for you because they might not be available when you need them. On the other hand, they're responsible for paying their own taxes, taking care of any benefits, such as health insurance, and using their own space and equipment, unless you agree to provide it. And you can find independent contractors in just about every industry and field.

Independent contractors are copywriters, web developers, accountants, lawyers, photographers, carpet cleaners, CD duplicators—whatever skill you need, an independent contractor can assist you.

Once you determine what skills you need to make your Etsy shop function more smoothly, you can post a brief job description on a local job board. If what you need is a quick one-time gig, you might want to give Fiverr (fiverr.com) a try. There are also freelance websites for many fields, from software coding to public relations to internet marketing.

Getting an Intern

If you could really use someone on a regular basis for a couple hours a day, or only a few hours per week, a high school or college intern may be a good fit for you. If the tasks you want to delegate include filing paperwork, for example, or packing and shipping sales, or answering questions via email, an intern may do the trick.

Many interns work for college credit instead of pay, as long as you provide more than just a clerical job. If you confirm you'll be teaching marketable skills, a college or university in the area may be willing to help find you some candidates. After you've determined the tasks you need completed regularly, call or email the career resource center or internship office at universities or colleges in your area. See if they have students who are looking for the kind of work you have, or if they can post your job for students to review.

You can also contact the chairman of a particular university department if your internship is primarily, say, marketing related or graphic design related. Sometimes professors can point you to their top students.

Some interns may ask to be paid, and you'll need to decide what your budget can handle. And if you can't afford to right now, be up front and let them know credit is all you can offer.

CRAFTY TOOLS

In your search for support services, a number of websites might help you identify potential candidates. Some of the best-known job search and freelance websites include Monster (monster.com), Elance (elance.com), Guru (guru.com), Indeed (indeed.com), Craigslist (craigslist.com), and LinkedIn (linkedin.com). Of course, use social media to alert your friends and colleagues to your hiring needs, too. Facebook is especially useful when you need someone on-site and can network with your local connections to see who might know someone.

Working with Family and Friends

Many start-up companies report relying on family and friends for financial and production support, but I caution you to think twice before you ask for help from those closest to you. One reason is that you may be offered advice you don't want or need, and you might feel pressured to take it if the advice-giver is lending you a hand.

Also, it can be hard to correct or reprimand a family member or friend who isn't working to your high standards. If you're not paying your dear ones, you might have a hard time getting them to value their work for you. So don't be surprised if little jobs you assign aren't done perfectly.

That doesn't mean you should never consider hiring family or friends—they can be life-savers when you're in a pinch. But if you're going to ask them to do important work for you, consider paying them for it and asking them to do it your way.

The Least You Need to Know

- Etsy has some of the best information sources and networks available to Etsy sellers—at no additional cost.

- One of Etsy's most helpful regular special reports is its Merchandising Report, which provides forecasts and trend data to help you decide where to invest your resources in creating new items for sale.

- Don't feel like you have to do everything your Etsy business requires yourself. Delegate the pieces you don't understand, or don't want to understand.

- Be careful about hiring friends and family to work in your business. They may have the best intentions, but you may not get the work done the way you want it unless you pay them.

Leveraging Etsy for Broader Success

In This Chapter

- Using Etsy to get noticed
- Focusing on the present
- Generosity fuels connections
- Using custom work as a try-out

Some crafters approach Etsy as the basis of their new business venture, while others find it can be so much more—even a stepping-stone to larger business opportunities. Either way, Etsy is one way to set up shop selling what you love, or to start to earn income from your passion or hobby, or to build a reputation in the arts community for what you do in the hopes it will lead to something more.

Until Etsy, many crafters could develop a local following, but becoming well known regionally or nationally was a long-shot. Now, with Etsy's international reach, garnering a national reputation is very possible.

So how do you position yourself to attract larger opportunities? Part of it's luck, as some Etsy sellers will tell you. Another factor is uniqueness. Are your pieces revolutionary or evolutionary? Revolutionary attracts more attention than a new version of something that already exists. If it's new and clever, you have a good chance of catching someone's eye, especially if you're investing any time in marketing.

In this chapter, you meet successful crafters who have used Etsy as a stepping-stone to bigger, more-lucrative opportunities.

Getting "Discovered"

Even if your long-term goal is larger than an Etsy shop, it's important to put your best effort into creating and building an impressive Etsy inventory and then promoting it as if your mortgage payment depended on it. Because if you take a half-hearted approach, always looking to the future rather than focusing on what's in front of you, it's unlikely your Etsy shop will do as well.

Bigger success generally comes from smaller successes, so do your best to be an Etsy success first.

You met plush artist Chris Hwang (ChrisCreatures) in an earlier chapter. She joined Etsy in January 2008 after reading a book on plush toys that inspired her to start sewing some of her own. Her pieces sold right away, and demand snowballed, especially after her Tofu for Obama plush, of which she sold hundreds. Her almost instant success on Etsy led to Hwang's work being accepted for the Crafty Bastards plush show, which then attracted invitations to art gallery shows and then bigger shows with bigger price points. At each level, Hwang raised her prices, moving from a $10 to $15 plush on Etsy to $100 pieces in galleries.

Thanks to her increasing exposure in the plush community, Hwang's work was featured in the plush magazine *Stuffed*. Today, Hwang is busier completing commissioned pieces than selling on Etsy, but if not for Etsy, she would never have been discovered and never had had all the opportunities that followed.

CRAFTY TOOLS

Although many artists worry about being too controversial or unique with their work, there's an upside to this. Going against the grain, or taking a crafty approach to a timely event, is one way to quickly get noticed. Don't always be safe. Being unconventional is often the first step to being noticed.

Positioning Yourself

What Hwang did well, and what you should aspire to do, is become known for something in particular—find your niche. Then, within your niche, create things others never have. Be trendy, if it appeals to you. Or innovative. But above all, be different, because doing what everyone else does will not position you for your big break. There's too much competition on Etsy for you to stand out if your pieces look too much like every other seller's.

Hwang wasn't trying to position herself for anything when she created her Tofu for Obama plush, but it was so cute and timely, her sales went through the roof. Other plush artists weren't as focused on creating election-themed pieces, so Hwang's item was a stand-out. The sales that followed pushed her into the forefront of her industry.

Being ahead of the pack positions you as an industry leader, which attracts attention from the media, which could then lead to new opportunities from businesses who are paying attention. So how do you get ahead of the pack?

Chapters 2 and 3 are all about studying the market, finding out what's selling now, and what's expected to sell in the future, so you may want to re-read them for ideas. That's what you need to know inside and out, as well as to decide how best to apply that information to what you love to do. If you hate politics, it's unlikely you'd enjoy brainstorming different ways to merge your craft with the election. So don't go there.

Instead, focus on something else that's trending—colors, textures, or price points—as well as upcoming events, whether it's Halloween or the much hoped-for birth of Prince William and Kate's first child.

Then, when you create something edgy or trendy or timely, you might want to renew the listing sooner than 4 months to get it to the top of the new listings page again. Ask for your Teams' help in including in treasuries. Feature it on your blog and in your Facebook and Twitter status updates. Be sure as many people as possible see it. That's the best way to generate buzz and attract attention that could lead somewhere new.

Increasing Your Odds

Being where the action is—on Etsy—is the best way to court new opportunities.

You met friends Hannah May Halleck and Deb Hepner earlier in the book, too. They began recycling shirts into knit skirts a few years ago. They buy colorful quality T-shirts at thrift stores and garage sales and transform them into unique skirts. At first, they just made skirts for themselves and wore them around town, until their friends saw the skirts and encouraged them to have home shows to sell them. The skirts flew off the racks.

To expand beyond their local area, the duo set up an Etsy shop (PrettyStinkinGreen), which became an instant hit. Through Etsy, the pair landed some wholesale accounts in Michigan and Illinois. A retailer in northern Michigan liked their work and asked for samples, which they sent and which she bought. Another Etsy customer bought a skirt and then asked about stocking more in her store, which further expanded their wholesale business.

To keep up with demand, and to ensure they are making a profit, the Pretty Stinkin' Green team has raised their prices a few times. At the start, their skirts sold for $30 and took about an hour to construct. Today, the skirts sell for $55 and up.

In addition to keeping their Etsy store constantly stocked, Hepner has worked to attract local media attention in Traverse City, Michigan. But again, success breeds success. Once they had one wholesale account, landing more was easier. However, Etsy remains a big profit center for them.

Making the Most of Your Etsy Connections

Your marketing plan might be focused on attracting buyers, but paying attention to fellow Etsy sellers may do even more for your business. Given the more than 800,000 sellers on Etsy, the power of the Etsy community is formidable. Imagine even a fraction of those sellers helping promote and support your business. The results could be overwhelming!

So why not invest some of your marketing time connecting with fellow sellers, rather than focusing so much on reeling in buyers? Yes, buyers are important, as are actual sales, but each Etsy seller might be worth four or five sales, through their buyers and connections, so your time may truly be better spent trying to establish relationships with people just like you.

Give Before You Ask

Etsy sellers may be your key to riches, but approaching them with a hand-out may not be well received. How do you feel when someone you don't know gets in touch asking you to do something for them, such as endorse them on LinkedIn or sending out a promotional email on their behalf? If you're most people, your knee-jerk reaction is to say, "Go away." So don't take this approach.

Rather than introducing yourself and asking for a favor, first offer something. Perhaps you can include one of their items in a treasury you're creating. Or ask if you can feature a photo of their work in your next blog post. Make their shop and an item a Favorite. Add them to your circle. Do something, anything they may perceive as a gesture of goodwill.

Offering to do something nice for someone else demonstrates your interest in their success and makes it much likelier they'll be willing to support yours.

Finding Support on Teams

Teams are built-in groups of potential supporters—fellow sellers who, like you, are working toward making money on Etsy. Members of these voluntary groups help each other and help themselves become more successful.

But because these groups are voluntary, the people who join are generally more committed to participating. That is, team members are frequently looking for ways to support other sellers, so your teams are the perfect place to start when looking to make connections with art galleries, catalogs, artists' agents, publishers, home furnishings manufacturers, and more.

CRAFTY TOOLS

All Etsy teams are run independent of the website, and some charge a fee to participate, to cover the cost of resources members have access to. For example, the Etsy Plush Team has 65 members from around the world who have applied and been accepted. They pay a fee, have access to a private Flickr group to share images, share gallery opportunities, and give each other support and critiques. By joining a team, Etsy sellers can tap into a wealth of contacts and experience.

Looking to Local Sellers

Just as your marketing program should include tactics that promote your crafts inside and outside Etsy, your efforts to pursue large opportunities should also involve Etsians and non-Etsians, such as artisans in your local area. One of Etsy's biggest advantages is its global marketplace, but its size and scope also make it harder to get noticed. Reaching out to and becoming part of local crafts groups makes good sense.

By participating in craft fairs and festivals, donating goods to local fund-raisers, joining local civic organizations and arts councils, and approaching area galleries and retailers about holding a show of your work, you can start to build a local fan base. That fan base can lead to customers and to other business opportunities.

Pursuing Commissions and Shows

Etsy cuts out the middleman, allowing crafters to sell directly to consumers, so price points are often lower than buyers see in traditional brick-and-mortar retailers. That's part of Etsy's appeal.

However, many sellers quickly find out it can be difficult to make a living when you're selling $15 or $20 items that took you an hour or more to create. That income ceiling is what often pushes Etsians to look for higher-earning opportunities beyond the website.

Considering Custom Work

Commissioned works, or custom-made projects, are frequently the gateways to larger-scale projects and income opportunities. By indicating in your shop that you welcome commissions, you're alerting customers that your skills go beyond what they see listed and that you can create almost anything they want that's similar to what you already have for sale.

A local interior designer in Rochester, New York, was helping an executive find artwork for his new office, so she turned to Etsy for options. She found the perfect painting, but it was much too small for the gentleman's office, so she contacted the artist to ask if she would consider creating a similar but larger version of her painting. The artist agreed and earned a fee that was multiples of what her smaller paintings sell for on Etsy.

Sometimes those opportunities present themselves simply because your work is a good fit for what a client wants or needs, which is impossible to predict. You just have to have a wide selection of your pieces in the public eye.

Highlighting Your Online Success

Commissions create additional opportunities to promote your skills. Be sure visitors see a photo of the commissioned work in a listing in your shop; mentioned in a blog post about your work; included in a status update on LinkedIn, Facebook, and Twitter; cited in an enewsletter article; and shared with all your teammates.

CRAFTY TOOLS

Many sellers post images of recent custom projects in an individual shop listing to show buyers what's possible. Simply create a listing showing a commissioned piece and what you charged for it as an example of what you *can* do. You can then update those photos as new custom projects come in, all for a total of $.60 a year. That may be the best advertising rate ever.

Word on the internet travels fast, so do all you can to keep your mailing list and connections well informed of your successes. That's the best way to attract even more success.

The Least You Need to Know

- Word of your success on Etsy starts to generate buzz, which gets more eyes on your shop—maybe a gallery owner or major client.
- The best way to find out about new business, media, and promotional opportunities is to join an active Etsy team in your niche.
- Before you start asking others to assist you, look for ways to offer your help and support.
- Getting hired to create a custom piece for a client is generally higher profit and higher visibility, which can lead to add-on work and commissions from other clients.
- When you finish a major project or do work for a big client, get their permission to share that news with your community of customers, fans, and colleagues.

break-even point   The price at which all your costs have been recouped, but you're not yet profitable. If your total cost to make a flower wreath is $18, for example, that's your break-even point. At $17.99, you're losing money, and at $18.01, you're making a profit. You always want to price your products above your break-even so you can generate a profit.

common law copyright   As an artist, your original design is protected by copyright the moment you create it. This is called a common law copyright. You should take additional steps to protect that copyright if anyone challenges it later (such as by filing official paperwork), but you earn it as soon as you create.

juried team   An Etsy team made of members who have had their workmanship and product photography reviewed before being accepted for inclusion on a team, much like an art exhibition. Juried teams are different from open teams because you have to apply and be accepted. *See also* team.

listing   A single item made available for sale on Etsy through the creation of a product page.

perceived value   The price a customer is willing to pay, regardless of what the product costs to produce. This pricing strategy works best with items in high demand or with art, where the unique qualities of handcrafted products make comparisons and substitutions virtually impossible.

public domain   The realm in which material is free and clear for the public to use. A literary work in the public domain, for example, doesn't need copyright protection, either because it expired or because it never had it. It can be modified and rereleased by other individuals or businesses at will.

statutory damages   Set fines imposed based on an incident, rather than calculated based on damages. Copyright infringement carries with it statutory damages of $30,000 per incident or $150,000 per incident if willful infringement is proven. The value of the item copied does not matter—the damages are the same.

tagging   A way for online sellers to attach keyword descriptions to products to help connect them with interested buyers. Tagging a cross necklace with terms like *gold*, *confirmation*, and *baptism*, for example, make it more likely the necklace will come up in a search for those same terms.

team   A group of Etsy sellers. Teams are formed with a primary goal of inspiring, encouraging, and promoting each other. You can't self-promote on Etsy, so joining a team gives you instant access to other people who agree to help promote your work. Etsy currently hosts more than 4,000 teams. Some are formed based on geography; some on crafting specialty; and others on gender, common interest, or level of experience. *See also* juried team.

treasury   A collection of 16 Etsy listings, generally around a central theme, sellers create to help promote each other. The treasuries are shown as a 4×4 square online. Some treasuries are selected for inclusion on the Etsy home page, which is a big draw.

trendspotting   Also called *trendwatching*, trendspotting is all about predicting the next big thing. Knowing what buyers will be looking for on Etsy in the coming weeks and months can help you decide how to invest your time crafting new items to list in your shop.

white box   A small box photographers use to control the amount of light surrounding a product they're photographing. They make photography at night and on dark days possible. You can buy or make white boxes fairly easily.

Resources

Blogger
blogger.com
A free tool for setting up and managing a blog.

Copyscape
copyscape.com
Check here to see if your website or product copy has been plagiarized.

Craft and Hobby Association
craftandHobby.org
The site can point you to trends and top crafters.

Craftcount
craftcount.com
This site ranks Etsy sellers by total sales, which can give you a sense of hot categories and point to Etsy sellers with a successful craft business.

Craftmonkey
craftmonkeyapp.com
This free mailing list service allows Etsy sellers to stay in touch with buyers using enewsletters.

Dwolla
dwolla.com
An alternative to PayPal, Dwolla charges lower fees for smaller amounts.

eBay
ebay.com
Search eBay for its most recent Hot List, which tells you which product categories are in high demand and which are cooling off. Enter "Hot List" at the Seller Information Center field and you'll be directed to recent hot lists, such as this one from Back to School 2012: pages.ebay.com/sellerinformation/sellingresources/2012/backtoschool.html.

EtsyText

etsytext.com

This free app texts you every time you make an Etsy sale, which can be especially helpful when you're on the road.

Facebook

facebook.com

The social media site allows you to post information about your Etsy shop on your personal Facebook page as well as on a business page.

Fiverr

fiverr.com

Buy or sell products or services for $5 here. It's an excellent source of extra help, especially with technical issues you don't know (or want to learn) how to address yourself.

Flickr

flickr.com

Flickr is one of the most popular sites Etsy sellers use to store, organize, and share images, so they don't clutter their computers.

FotoFuze

fotofuze.com

This photography tool makes it simpler and easier to change the background of any product photo to white.

FreeDigitalPhotos.net

freedigitalphotos.net

This stock photo website provides royalty-free images, meaning images you don't need to pay to use.

Google AdWords Keyword Tool

adwords.google.com/o/KeywordTool

This online tool identifies which words are used more frequently in online searches.

Google Trends

google.com/trends

Check this page to see the most popular searched-for terms on Google.

Internal Revenue Service

irs.gov

The IRS's official website provides downloadable tax forms.

Internships.com

internships.com

This website helps link organizations in need of interns with students looking for learning opportunities.

LinkedIn

linkedin.com

Many professionals use this social media site to network and share information.

MAKE Blog

blog.makezine.com

This blog offers a free tutorial on making a photographic white box for little or no money.

PayPal

paypal.com

This online payment system enables you to collect electronic payment from buyers almost instantaneously.

Pinterest

pinterest.com

At this visual website, members can share images and videos of products and projects for inspiration and information.

PublicityInsider.com

publicityinsider.com

Check this site for helpful tips on preparing press releases and other media relations tools.

Skinny Artist

skinnyartist.com

This site's tutorial on shrink-wrapping and on watermarking your images can help protect them from being stolen.

SkipMcGrath's Online Seller's Resource

skipmcgrath.com

This eBay guru has a link to each state's sales tax rates on a page at his site.

Square

square.com

This payment system enables you to accept credit cards remotely using your smartphone.

SurveyMonkey

surveymonkey.com

This online market research tool enables you to conduct surveys via email. Basic surveys are free.

TinEye

tineye.com

TinEye does for images what Copyscape does for words, searching for unauthorized use of images you own.

TraxTime

spudcity.com/traxtime

This time-tracking software package available from SpudCity enables you to carefully monitor your time spent on various aspects of your Etsy business to ensure your prices reflect how much time you've invested.

Twitpic

twitpic.com

This app allows you to take a photo and tweet about it.

Twitter

twitter.com

Twitter is a social media tool that allows you to provide 140-character status reports to your followers list.

U.S. Copyright Office

copyright.gov

At the U.S. government copyright office's website, you can file a copyright application or learn more about how to protect yourself from copyright infringement.

U.S. Postal Service

usps.gov

At the U.S. Postal Service's site, you can request free shipping supplies for Priority and Express Mail packages, arrange for pick-ups, and track packages.

WePay

wepay.com

This PayPal alternative carries lower fees.

WordPress

wordpress.com

This blogging tool has become the new standard in blogging and website creation. There's a free version and a paid version.

Yahoo! Groups

groups.yahoo.com

Join Yahoo! Groups to find other Etsy sellers or crafters interested in networking and sharing information.

Index

U-V

W-X-Y-Z

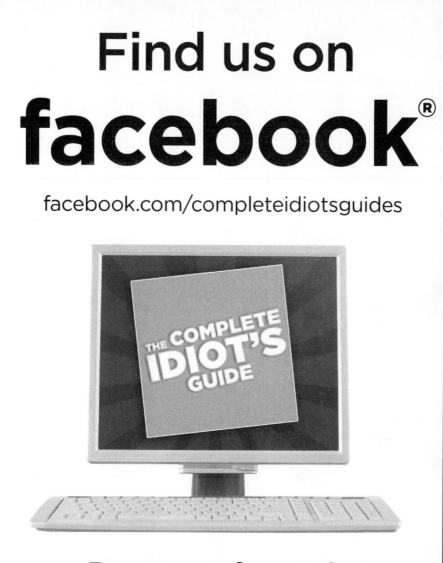

CHECK OUT T
BEST-SELL

More than 450 titles available at booksellers and onl

THE COMPLETE IDIOT'S GUIDE TO Rights and wrongs of sentence structure, word usage, spelling, and much more

Grammar & Style
Laurie E. Rozakis, Ph.D.

978-1-59257-115-4

THE COMPLETE IDIOT'S GUIDE TO 301 twisters and teasers for a stimulating mental workout

Word Search Puzzles
Matt Gaffney

978-1-59257-900-6

THE COMPLETE IDIOT'S GUIDE TO Rev up your metabolism and lose weight—for good

Glycemic Index Weight Loss
SECOND EDITION
Lucy Beale and Joan Clark-Warner, M.S., R.D., C.D.E.

978-1-59257-855-9

THE COMPLETE IDIOT'S GUIDE TO A revealing comparison of the faiths that shape the lives of millions

World Religions
FOURTH EDITION
Brandon Toropov and Father Luke Buckles

978-1-61564-069-0

THE COMPLETE IDIOT'S GUIDE TO Give your resume a professional makeover—and stand out from the pack

The Perfect Resume
FIFTH EDITION
Susan Ireland

978-1-59257-957-0

THE COMPLETE IDIOT'S GUIDE TO A lively, comprehensive guide to the dramatic history of our great nation

American History
FIFTH EDITION
Alan Axelrod, Ph.D.

978-1-59257-869-6

THE COMPLETE IDIOT'S GUIDE TO Sail through class with foolproof explanations and dozens of practice problems

Calculus
SECOND EDITION
W. Michael Kelley

978-1-59257-471-1

THE COMPLETE IDIOT'S GUIDE TO Easy, effective, and enjoyable methods for you and your dog

Positive Dog Training
Pamela Dennison

978-1-61564-066-9

THE COMPLETE IDIOT'S GUIDE TO Money-management tips and investment strategies to put your money in your pocket

Personal Finance in Your 20s & 30s
FOURTH EDITION
Sarah Young Fisher and Susan Shelly

978-1-59257-883-2

THE COMPLETE IDIOT'S GUIDE TO Tips and tricks to getting your house in order—one room at a time

Organizing Your Life
FIFTH EDITION
Georgene Lockwood

978-1-59257-966-2

CD INCLUDED!
THE COMPLETE IDIOT'S GUIDE TO Audio exercises let you listen, learn, and practice.

Learning Spanish
FIFTH EDITION
Step-by-step lessons help you speak Spanish like a native
Gail Stein

978-1-59257-908-2

THE COMPLETE IDIOT'S GUIDE TO Refine your taste for the finest in vino

Wine Basics
SECOND EDITION
Tara Q. Thomas

978-1-59257-786-6

THE COMPLETE IDIOT'S GUIDE TO Make friends with the social network

Facebook®
SECOND EDITION
Mikal E. Belicove and Joe Kraynak

978-1-61564-118-5

CD INCLUDED!
THE COMPLETE IDIOT'S GUIDE TO Audio CD The Complete Idiot's Guide Ear Training Course

Music Theory
SECOND EDITION
Michael Miller

978-1-59257-437-7

THE COMPLETE IDIOT'S GUIDE TO

Walt Disney World
2012 EDITION
Doug Ingersoll

978-1-61564-112-3

ALPHA
idiotsguides.com